CHRIST

THE AVATAR OF SACRIFICIAL LOVE

TORKOM SARAYDARIAN

Aquarian Educational Group
P.O. Box 267 · Sedona, AZ 86339

Christ, The Avatar of Sacrificial Love
First Printing 1974 ©1974 by H. Saraydarian
Second Printing 1994 ©1994 The Creative Trust

All Rights Reserved: No part of this publication may be reproduced, stored in a retrieval system, or transmitted in any form, by any means, electronic, mechanical, photocopying, recording or otherwise, without the permission in writing from the copyright owner or representatives designated by the copyright owner.

ISBN: 0-911794-70-0 hardcover
        0-911794-69-7 softcover

Library of Congress Catalog Number: 74-11760

Printed in the United States of America

Cover Design: *Fine Point Graphics*
                Sedona, Arizona

Printed by: *DATA Reproductions Corporation*
                Rochester Hills, Michigan

Published by: **Aquarian Educational Group**
                P.O. Box 267
                Sedona, Arizona 86339
                United States of America

Note: *The exercises and meditations contained in this book are given as guidelines. They should be used with discretion and after receiving professional advice.*

Dedicated to
MASTER
K.H.

▲

The Spirit of Christ breathes across the
 desert of life.
Like a spring It wears Its way through the
 solid rocks.
In the milky firmament It radiates in myriads of
 lights, and rises upward in the stems of
 flowers.

▲

We lay stones for the steps of the resplendent
 Temple.
In the name of Christ we carry the rocks.
Erect Thy altar, O Lord, in our garden.
The rocks are too large for the garden.
Too steep the steps for the flowers.
On a cloud He approaches.
On the grass shall He sit beside us.
I rejoice, O Lord, to give to Thee my
 garden.
Depart not, O Manifested Lord.
Desert not our garden.
With stars is Thy Path adorned.
Among them shall I find Thy Way.
I shall follow Thee — My Lord.
Should the worldly sun disperse
Thy starry signs,
Then shall I invoke the aid of storm and wave to
 veil its rays.
Wherein its use if it obscure Thy starry tokens?

CONTENTS

	A FEW WORDS	9
1	THE TORCH OF THE AGES	11
2	FORMATION OF THE PLAN	15
3	CYCLIC APPEARANCES	29
4	MARY	33
5	THE GLORIOUS SUNRISE	39
6	THE THREE MAGI OR THE KINGS	51
7	PREPARATION	55
8	THROUGH MANY LANDS	63
9	IN THE PAST	73
10	THE CHRIST	83
11	IN THE WILDERNESS	89
12	INITIATIONS	97
13	HIS TEACHING IN PALESTINE	113
14	THE UPPER ROOM	123
15	GETHSEMANE	137
16	JESUS AND APOLLONIUS	141
17	JUDAS THE ISCARIOT	161
18	MASTER JESUS — PRESENT AND FUTURE	165
19	RENDING THE VEILS	169
20	CONTEMPORARY WORK OF THE CHRIST	181
21	THE CHRIST TODAY	197
22	CHRIST IN THE IMMEDIATE FUTURE	203
23	THE WAY TO CHRIST	217
24	APOSTOLIC SUCCESSION	255
23	THE TEACHING OF CHRIST	257
	INDEX	279
	ABOUT THE AUTHOR	295

A Few Words

This book is not written for average Christians, for those who are lost in "Churchianity" or in social-religious activities, with their narrow-minded views, doctrines and dogmas, interests, and, worst of all, with their hatreds.

This book is written for those who can see a great beauty in Christ and try to express that beauty by living a life of sacrificial love.

We know about those aberrated "Christians" and other religious fanatics who, "following after the steps of Christ" or of their prophet, shed the blood of millions and millions of people, even up to the twentieth century. We remember the Inquisitors. We remember the wars between various churches. We remember and even see in this age the hatred that exists among Christians and other religions. We know how churches have exploited the name of that purest Soul, Who came to teach Love, Sacrifice, Simplicity, Beauty, and Spirituality.

This book is a bouquet of flowers offered at His Sacred Feet.

Torkom Saraydarian

1

▲ The Torch of the Ages ▲

The day when man for the first time felt that the whole creation was the work of a great Architect, that day a window was opened toward the Cosmos, toward the future possibilities, toward the Future itself.

Unfolding souls, as they progressed upon the Path, felt not only the Hand of a Creator, but they also saw order and harmony in the creation. They heard the hidden symphony reverberating in all the galaxies, in all systems, in all globes, even in each atom.

They saw a unity in all creation, a creation which was not a machine but an organism, every part of which was a living part with its special role to play in the totality of creation.

These Great Ones respected Nature as a great Mother, and They saw in every living form an unfolding Plan. They loved animals, birds, the lilies in the field, human beings, and They sang great songs of gratitude to the oceans, to the lakes, to the blue skies, to the rain, knowing that all these living forms were ultimately necessary to carry on the sacred Purpose of the Creator.

Ages came and ages passed, and these Great Ones left Their songs as guiding lights for humanity.

They taught the Law of Goodness, the Law of Beauty, the Laws of Truth, Simplicity, and Fearlessness. They taught us to abide in faith, in hope, and in love. The faith They taught was an innate, intuitive comprehension of the beauty, goodness, and truth in all creation.

Hope was the response in man to the Great Magnet which draws each Spark back Home. Love was the communion with the Almighty Presence in each living form.

Those who saw this vision, the great blueprint which was the mystic symphony behind the creation, became like blooming flowers, blooming trees, and entered into a greater communication with the Heart of the Creator to further His Purpose according to His Plan and make the symphony heard within each atom.

One of them was a fiery Soul Who, for the first time in the history of the human race, entered into Enlightenment. He stood in the presence of that mysterious Being Who is called the Ancient of Days, Melchizedek, the One Initiator, or Sanat Kumara.

Thus He opened a conscious line of communication between that great station of Power, Love, and Beauty and struggling humanity. He became a bridge, and in the stormy and dark oceans of the life of humanity the compass was found, the North Star was seen. Hope was spread in the hearts of the sons of men . . . and the Purpose of creation was sensed.

Many, many millions of years ago, He was a youth Who developed a love of philosophy in His heart. He found the way to *think*, to hear the great hidden call through each form, to sense the pull of the great Cosmic Heart. Throughout ages, His intention was to enter into closer communication with the Mind behind the phenomenal universe.

He passed through all human sufferings, and as He pressed forward for more light, for more love, the heavy clouds of human ignorance broke their thunder on His body and heart.... But He never gave up. He was running His marathon race upon the planet, and He decided never to stop at any cost but to press forward to the Good.

As He traveled the path of pain, the path of sacrifice and service, the great flower of compassion flourished in His heart and eventually embraced the whole planet.

In the dark deserts of human consciousness, He shone as a torch of fire. Because of His ageless service and unceasing sacrifices, He became the Senior Member of the invisible Temple, of the invisible Church, to guide humanity from darkness to light.

Age after age, He reappeared among men, giving the same Teaching, opening the same Way, and expressing the same Beauty.

All those who responded through their life, service, and sacrifice gathered around Him, and the Center of Love grew and grew, becoming a fiery Magnet attracting the Cosmic Energies, the Cosmic Beauties.

It is from this Center that all Saviors throughout the ages and in all countries went forth, taking with Them the message of Compassion, the message of Beauty, Service, Sacrifice, Simplicity, and Fearlessness.

We are told that He is on the way back to the world of men to renew in our hearts a greater hope, a greater faith, and a greater love.

2

▲ Formation of The Plan ▲

WHEN THIS PLANET was created by the Great Entity, called the Solar Logos in ancient esoteric books, and when it was ensouled by the Planetary Logos, we are told They had a great Purpose which, as a seed, was destined to grow and unfold to become a Cosmic Beauty in Space.

This Purpose was translated into a great Plan by the Enlightened Ones and was partially passed on to humanity in the form of world religions, philosophies, yogas, and mysteries. Those who were able to sense and respond to this great Plan were those who had a great vision for the future of all living forms.

This vision was to be for ages and ages, throughout which the scattered Sparks were going to unfold from kingdom to kingdom and gradually enter into their solar and Cosmic destinations.

For this purpose the great Initiator organized an advanced, central group on this planet with great Beings to study the *Will* of the Solar Life and to formulate it into a Plan in order to further that Purpose to its last point of fulfillment. In occult books this event is called the Founding of the Hierarchy on our planet Earth.

The founding of the Hierarchy occurred many millions of years after the individualization of humans began. This Center was formed by advanced Beings Who came with Sanat Kumara from another chain in our scheme[1]. Their plan was to expand the consciousness of humanity and through education make its brain sensitive to the Plan. Then gradually humanity, too, would be able to understand the Purpose of the Planetary Logos. Initially, all the members of this Center were extra-planetary Beings, but as time went on advancing human beings entered the Hierarchy and replaced Those Who were ready to depart. We are told that at this time the members of Hierarchy are graduates from humanity.

The great Beings Who came from certain planetary chains and formed our Hierarchy were men of great power and knowledge. In the *Bible* and in other esoteric literature They were called Gods, or Sons of God. The *Bible* says that the Sons of God walked with the children of men and even married the daughters of men. They were very advanced Beings from previous *manvantaras*[2] and were called upon to help with the progress of humanity on its path toward Cosmic evolution.

We can find the echoes of advanced Beings in the mythology of all nations — in Asia, in Europe, in America, and in all parts of the world. These Great Ones brought to humanity statesmanship, education,

---

[1] See *Cosmos in Man* by Torkom Saraydarian, pp. 25-31.
[2] Read *Ibid.*, pp. 71-72.

▲ FORMATION OF THE PLAN ▲ 17

philosophy, the arts, the sciences, religions, and mysteries (or rituals and ceremonies), guiding humans toward self-actualization.

The Great Ones possessed well-developed minds, an unfolded heart nature, and powerful will energy. Their main obligation was to penetrate into the Purpose, into the Will of the Almighty One, *see* it, and then bring it down to the human level and try to lead humanity according to what They saw of the Purpose of the Great One. Their spiritual contact with the Purpose of God created, on the Intuitional Plane and in Their higher minds, a mighty thoughtform, a great blueprint, which later was called the Plan for this planet.

This Plan was not only for humanity but for all kingdoms — mineral, vegetable, animal, and human — and even for the super-human kingdom, the fifth kingdom, the kingdom of Souls.

The Great Ones believed that, because of the level of human understanding at that time, this Plan could be given or presented to humanity in part through symbolic dances, dramas, symbols, rituals, ceremonies, and worship.

They first created a great drama in the Hierarchy itself and enacted it to see whether They could reflect in this drama the immediate Purpose of God. They based this drama on the blueprints of a Cosmic drama which was and is taking place on solar and Cosmic scales, and which is called the drama of Cyclic Revelation of the Great Mystery.

They created this drama with its colors, numbers, music, chants, rituals, and symbols in such a way that They could gradually unveil and unfold the great mystery as the consciousness of man expanded, age after age, through experience, suffering, and learning.

They divided their symbolic play into seven sections, as the seven rays of the Sun, but started to demonstrate them first through educational and religious dramas, endeavoring to make the advancing members of humanity aware of a hidden mystery behind the phenomenal Universe and to teach them how to approach that mystery individually and in group formation.

According to the esoteric Science of the Rays, our solar system is a Second Ray system, which means a Love-Wisdom system. The Second Ray corresponds to World Education. Religion falls into the Sixth Ray approach, which is that of devotion, aspiration, initiating causes, and the creation of duality, vision, and sacrifice for a greater goal.

The Great Ones tried first to reach humanity by these two channels. So the Hierarchy of advanced Masters sent out Their own members into the world to start and to establish, wherever possible, centers of education and centers of worship through lesser and greater mysteries. In these mysteries was hidden the whole knowledge of the science of becoming Oneself, which touched the core of the divine Purpose.

Thus, the mystery schools were created in Egypt, in Armenia, in Greece, Syria, Palestine, India, Tibet, Mongolia, and in Central and South America.

The mysteries were great visions that the Hierarchy wanted to impress upon the minds of the candidates for initiation. The ceremonials and rituals were scientific processes to transmute and transform the nature of man and to enable him to stand within the greater light of a greater revelation.

▲ FORMATION OF THE PLAN ▲ 19

Each mystery, each symbol was created in such a way that it would keep changing its depth and its implications, and gradually it was translated by the initiate on the levels of humanity, the planet, the solar system, and the Cosmic field.

Students of anthropology and religion will have no difficulty in tracing the path of evolution and the extension of the mystery schools throughout the world. Behind all these mystery schools there existed one central Core — the Hierarchy — from which streamed forth great educators and leaders, carrying out to the shores of human consciousness the life-giving waves of Their Teachings of order, law, education, light, beauty, knowledge, ceremonies, and rituals through the medium of sacred temple dances, music, words, and colors.

These greater and lesser mysteries had a profound effect upon the consciousness of man, and as years passed they created a great aspiration for upliftment, for right human relations, for a sense of beauty, for simplicity and harmony, and a great thirst for knowledge and service.

The Hierarchy was built upon a foundation of organized labor. The achievement of each member of the Hierarchy is the result of long-range, sacrificial labor, extending over countless incarnations.

Every disciple who feels the urge to become a co-worker with the Hierarchy and take responsibilities in the ranks of the Hierarchy must be an embodiment of labor and, as a great magnet, attract those who respond to his call to labor.

The members of the Hierarchy are organizers of great labors. It is only through labor and, eventually, through sacrificial labor that the Spark of Will Power awakens in man and drives him forward toward the integration of his bodies, toward alignment with his spiritual nature, and toward soul and monadic fusion.

Striving is the process of response of the awakening fire of the Will to the call of labor on higher and higher planes. All those who work within the aura of the Hierarchy are organizers of great labors. Their goal is to build the Inner Sanctuary within the pyramid, the Spiritual Triad.

You can see an example of this labor in the process of construction of the great pyramid of Egypt. This massive monument, four hundred and eighty-two feet high, is based on a foundation seven hundred and sixty-eight feet square. Two million, three hundred thousand stones, each weighing two and one-half tons, were used in its construction. A historian of the ancient world concluded that one hundred thousand men worked twenty years to erect this marvel. The important aspect of this great undertaking was not only the enormous amount of labor provided for one hundred thousand people, but also the growth and development achieved by the workers through their life-long labor. It provided strong discipline and the reorientation and polarization of their forces, energies, thoughts, and ideas toward a great achievement, a vision which was coming into reality. It was through such labor that the wise hierarchical engineers of that time caused a tremendous transmutation within the physical, emotional, and mental bodies of the masses, leading them to a higher stage of evolution and to a greater depth of understanding of the Universe.

Those who really learned to labor with vision, sacrifice, understanding, and cooperation were those

▲ Formation of The Plan ▲ 21

disciples who were to be initiated into the greater mysteries within the king's chamber of the pyramid.
This same must also be true for our modern world. Wherever advanced culture is found, we find a great labor to move forward toward higher steps of evolution. Hence, the organized labor of great projects in any department of human endeavor is a liberating, integrating, and transforming process for all those who are wholeheartedly involved in them.

The members of the Hierarchy and Their disciples are those who have graduated from great labors on physical, emotional, and mental levels and whose intention now is to build better bridges and communication lines between man and greater units of life, to bring universal and Cosmic energies to the lower kingdoms, and to unite them for greater labor. Through labor a flower blooms, through labor a Christ is, through labor a planet sustains life, through labor the sun shines, through labor the stars and galaxies proceed.

The life of each form, of each atom and each cell, has the innate drive to go forward to higher spheres of evolution to become a part of higher organisms upon higher planes. The tiny life in the physical atom does not remain forever as a part of one system in the physical body. It proceeds to higher systems and graduates from the pineal gland to the astral body, becoming a part of that body. When it graduates from the astral body, it enters into the mental body, then becomes a part of the higher mental body, and so on until one day it forms a center by itself in a life form.

The same thing happens to the human unit. On the path of evolution, when he has graduated from physical, astral, and lower mental planes, man becomes an atom in the body of a greater life. He then proceeds with his evolution and eventually becomes an atom of the centers of the Planetary Logos, the Solar Logos, and eventually a part of Their Chalices.

Thus he learns the mystery of group life, individualizing himself from a lower life and subordinating himself to a higher life through greater awareness and in greater harmony with the whole.

We are told that the centers of Great Lives are formed of the kingdoms of Nature; higher centers are formed of higher Initiates; and the highest centers are formed of Masters, Chohans, and greater Avatars. How wonderful to imagine that as a group of atoms succeeds in forming either our brain or an etheric center in our subtle body, so a group of people, traveling together throughout ages, will one day form a lotus in the body of a *Heavenly Man.*

Some of the great Teachers Who appeared among humanity built the pyramids. Some of Them built the great temples in Greece and India. They were very advanced architects, musicians, dancers, and poets. They knew the science of sound and color by which They built most of Their temples. When They started to build these temples, They also initiated baby humanity into the ABC's of the mysteries of love, understanding, and right human relations. Then slowly, as ages passed, a few disciples made the degree and were initiated into greater mysteries. The first Great One to achieve Mastership was the Christ.

Throughout ages very advanced Souls, such as Vyasa, Hermes, Hercules, Zoroaster, Confucius, Plato, Jesus, and others were sent out from the Hierarchy. Most of Them were from our own humanity. Wherever

▲ FORMATION OF THE PLAN ▲ 23

They went, They taught the great Teachings of the Hierarchy, and They created great friction, upheavals, revolutions, and wars. Most of these great beings had been warriors and captains of armies in past incarnations, and some had been high executives in government.

Whenever light or power strikes someone, it causes friction until that person is able to digest and assimilate it or until he rejects it. If he rejects that light and that opportunity, he will have to wait for another cycle until a similar opportunity occurs. That is why Jesus said, "I came to bring the sword, not peace." The great Teachers wanted to shake the mass of humanity out of its lethargy to clean and awaken it. Those of you who read about the mysteries will see that these mysteries were a process of purification — physically, emotionally, mentally — through suffering, through baptism, and through burning, the intense burning of aspiration.

As centuries passed, these Teachers revealed more and more of the mysteries of the Teaching, and, as the disciples began to advance, they were given more of the mysteries and were taken into more advanced initiations. These mysteries were given in the temples in secret, mainly in the form of dramas so that people could look at them, understand them, digest them, and then build their own lives based on the meanings behind those mysteries.

Christ was part of the Hierarchy, and it was He Who decided to enact a part in the Cosmic drama of Revelation on the stage of the world with actual living beings, actual blood, tears, and sacrifice to demonstrate to humanity the path toward a supreme revelation. This was a heroic decision, and upon this decision He was granted permission to unveil this drama to the world. Before He started to enact His mysteries in front of humanity, He chose age after age all His actors and trained them in the actual ways of life, tested them in all levels of their nature, galvanized them with His power of Love, and sent them to earth through actual birth, one by one, to the place where He was going to demonstrate the live drama of Cosmic Revelation.

Because of His human origin and because of His power of illumination and achievement, Christ became a bridge between the great Mystery and humanity and called Himself "the Truth, the Path, and the Life."

One of the Enlightened Sons of God said that Christ worked so hard throughout the ages, sacrificed so much, and tried to live His life so close to the divine Plan for man that He became, in a sense, the embodiment or a progressively unfolding embodiment or symbol of the Plan. Like a magnet, He drew to Himself all those who were sensitive enough to His call and willing to pass consciously the discipline of daily life in the light of that divine Magnet. They stood by His side for Cosmic evolution, sharing with Him all powers of inner divinity and all authority over the lower kingdoms in Nature.

As a man advances, he becomes a center that draws more energy from Cosmic sources. He becomes a transmitter and also a sort of refinery which purifies the etheric, emotional, and mental spheres, burning in them the dross of wrong human activities, negative emotions, mental illusions, and ugly thoughtforms. When this occurs with a group of men, they form a great Magnet which draws energy from Cosmic sources. After a long period of appropriation and assimilation, this energy is channeled to humanity, allowing awakening souls of men to see the light and take beginning steps toward the Plan through a process of steady discipline and service.

We must be very grateful to these men and women. Through their achievements they create a rarified and magnetic field in the atmosphere through which the blessing of the higher spheres precipitates upon the world, creating at times an intense purification and blooming. They bring beauty and the fire of pure striving toward the Great Future.

When such people exist within humanity, because of their advanced knowledge they create a broadcasting station on the mental plane to transmit to humanity the wealth and beauty of divine knowledge. Those who have subtle antennas will eventually tune in to such stations and tremendously enrich their own lives and those of others with great inspiration and creativity.

Most of our advanced artists and scientists are in touch with these centers through their antahkarana[1] or "antenna," and what they bring to the world is the precipitation of the "cloud of knowable things," as these energy fields are called in the Ageless Wisdom.

We can say that they not only bring inspiration and knowledge to humanity but, because of their very existence, they also act as transmuting agents within humanity.

It would be very difficult and would take many more millions of years for humanity to arrive at its present stage were it not for the great sacrificial service of these perfected souls.

---

[1] Read *The Science of Becoming Oneself* by Torkom Saraydarian, Ch. XVIII.

Our planet, because of a big failure that took place on the moon, was delayed millions of years on the Cosmic timetable. The Great Ones had to take drastic steps to bring our planet to the necessary degree for harmony with solar progress. The Hierarchy eventually established seven centers on the planet. Through these seven centers the solar energy, or the higher love and understanding, started to circulate.

The Great Ones magnetized seven places on the planet with Their personal blessings. Huge stones, temples, and even big trees and forests were blessed and charged with magnetic energy so that solar energies could be attracted and spread through these charged objects. Whatever They touched, wherever They walked, They created a whirlpool of magnetic energy. It is at these locations that spiritual blooming, culture, and civilization started through educational institutions, temples, and palaces.

The Great Ones came like waves of the ocean, cyclically and rhythmically. In every age, great Sons of Light visited humanity to repeat the mysteries on an ever deeper level, giving greater symbols to evoke a greater light from the minds of men.

Mysteries are formed by symbolic signs and ceremonies. Symbols protect us from premature understanding of divine laws and divine knowledge. They unveil themselves as our consciousness expands due to our study, discipline, and service.

The unfoldment of the symbols continues until the day when a master mind reads in them the original Purpose of the Great Mind of the solar system.

That is why genuine symbols never die away, and in every age the interest shown toward them increases and the interpretation deepens.

The basic intention of the mysteries was to release the spark from the prison of the Cosmic Physical Plane and to gradually unfold its latent power to enable it to reach the Source from whence it came.

3

▲ Cyclic Appearances ▲

It is amazing to notice that all the Great Ones Who visited the earth gave the same message, according to the level of the people and the conditions of life.

We see a very close similarity in Their language of symbolism, the major life events through which They passed, and even similarities in Their births, struggles, services, deaths, and victories.

In the history of world religion you can find the names of Great Ones, and parts of Their message are scattered throughout the pages of tradition, from east to west, from north to south, in all ages.

Most of Them were born at the winter solstice of virgin mothers who were endowed with great virtue, wisdom, and power.

Each time They appeared, They came to meet a human need. In *The Bhagavad Gita* we are told that They appear *whenever men become indifferent toward their duties and responsibilities, and whenever unrighteousness and disorder increase . . . to protect the virtuous, to destroy the wicked, and to re-establish the sense of duty and responsibility. . . .*[1]

We see in all ages that the message of the great Teachers gradually loses its true note and is eventually used for human vanities.

We are told that every time a great Teacher came to the world, He faced dark crystallizations and wide degeneration of the Teaching. His main task became to stress the simplicity and the beauty of the Teaching in real fearlessness.

When any crystallization and degeneration occur in the Teaching, they become the worst enemies to the new Teaching. They prevent the possibility of a new revelation that the same Teaching might take. The new Teaching immediately mobilizes its enemies who fight against it until it loses its original purity and starts to crystallize. Immediately after such a crystallization, the persecution stops and the Teaching serves to increase the vanities of the so-called teachers who acquire great wealth, high positions, authority, dogmas, and doctrines.

Although this continues age after age, it does not mean that the Teaching has failed. Every time it hits the shores of human consciousness, it draws to itself awakened Sons of Light, initiating them into simplicity, beauty, and fearlessness. This is how, one by one, here

---

[1] *The Bhagavad Gita* 4:7-8, Torkom Saraydarian, tr.

and there, dedicated souls enter into the Holy Place and join the Hierarchy of Light.

At the time Jesus was born, conditions in the civilized world were at their worst. The Teaching and the mystery religions were crystallized, and they were being used to exploit the poor and the innocent. The political field was full of corruption, and the morals of the majority were very low. People were only after physical and emotional satisfaction through the misuse of energy, power, and authority.

The progress of humanity was in danger. Advanced souls cannot reincarnate and hold positions in a world that runs in corruption and crime, dominated by low urges and drives. Then, when the birth of such souls is prevented, the progress of humanity slows down and stops.

Even in rare cases in which advanced souls were able to be born, they found insurmountable difficulties on their path, and eventually they found themselves under the command of the forces of materialism, selfishness, and fear. Only Chosen Ones Who have the shield of Hierarchy can survive and shed Their light in spite of conditions and the attacks by the dark forces.

We are told that at that time

> ... the civilized world plunged into an indescribable orgy of immorality, treachery, and wickedness. Rome, the greatest world-power of that time, was the center of debauchery and evil intrigue. It had conquered Palestine in 63 B.C. In the next decade came the rapid rise to power of Julius Caesar, and in 49 B.C. occurred the civil war with Pompey, in which the latter was victorious. Pompey appointed Herod

as governor of Galilee and Jerusalem. Herod, in 20 B.C. had his wife Marianne put to death, and in 6 B.C., growing suspicious of the ambitions of his sons, he had them both strangled....
 ...Anthony and Cleopatra met their tragic end in the year 30 B.C.
 Selfishness, egotism, and animalism reigned supreme. The life of average humanity was so evil that almost the entire period of the after-death state was spent in the purgatorial regions with little or no time for the heaven-world experience. Human evolution had come almost to a standstill.
 Herod the Great died in 4 B.C. and was succeeded by his son, Herod Antipas.... He attempted extermination of all things that were virtuous and holy. The spiritual life of the world was at low ebb.[1]

It was under such conditions that Jesus was sent to be the vehicle of a great Spirit and Light and to protect the Teaching of the Hierarchy and the Path of Salvation of humanity.

---

[1] Heline, Corinne, *The New Age Bible Interpretation, The New Testament.*

4

▲ Mary ▲

THERE ARE BEAUTIFUL, traditional stories which have great meaning and are part of the great drama which Christ is going to enact.

Each person in these stories is playing a role to unveil the great meaning and purpose behind the drama. The actors slowly will appear on the stage and perform their duties.

Not all of them are conscious of the roles they are playing, but as the drama unfolds they begin to see the great beauty behind it — such a great beauty that they easily give their lives to perpetuate that beauty.

A shepherd lived in Palestine who was a very rich old man and who had in his heart the spirit of God, the spirit of goodwill. His name was Joachim. He had a wife, and her name was Anna.

Tradition says that the mother of Mary was a Princess. Her name was Grapte of Kharax, a cousin of Queen Helena of Adiabene. She was betrothed to marry her cousin Nakeeb. He was a prince of the province of

Adiabene and a descendant of the ancient royal family of Media. They became proselytes into Judaism, and because of their wealth and social position they were very close to the ruling classes in Jerusalem. After they were converted, they were called Anna and Joachim.

Many stories in the *New Testament* are distorted deliberately to make Jesus one of the descendants of King David. The learned and ruling classes were aware of this distortion. Hence they rejected Him.

Joachim lived with his wife for twenty years, and they had no children. At the time of a great Feast of Dedication, Joachim took gifts to the Temple to dedicate them and to sacrifice them to God. But, when he entered the Temple, the High Priest told him that he was not to bring any gift to the Almighty One because he was not blessed with children, and he was referred to as "a barren tree." He was informed that his offerings could never be acceptable to God, Who had judged him unworthy of having children.

This was a great shame for Joachim. He took his gifts, and in great sorrow and pain he left the Temple and went home. For three days he cried with his wife. A few days later he decided to leave the village, and, taking his flocks, he went far away into the mountains to live there with his sorrow.

Tradition says that eventually he decided to fast for forty days and pray to the Lord. His wife at home came to the same decision. She shut herself in her house and began to fast and pray.

One day when she was sitting under a tree, she saw that a little sparrow was building a nest for the eggs it would lay. She watched the sparrow busily engaged in its work, and suddenly she burst into tears, crying, "My

Lord, you have given a nest to this little creature in which to lay its eggs and to have its offspring, but why have you forsaken me?"

While she was in tears and sorrow, she felt a presence around her. Looking up she saw a flaming angel beside her who said, "Very soon your tears will be wiped away, and again joy will dwell in your heart. Your husband has decided to come back. Now get ready to go and meet him at the big gate of the city, and the same day you are going to conceive and have a daughter."

When the angel disappeared, Anna left the house in great joy and went to the big gate. She waited for hours, but no one appeared. At sunset, in tears, she decided to go home.

As she set her face toward home, she felt two strong hands take hold of her shoulders and a male voice said, "Anna, you were waiting for me. The Angel of the Lord appeared to me in the mountains and told me to come back and meet you here.

"He said to me, 'Your prayers are heard, and your alms have ascended in the sight of God. . . . Anna, your wife, will bring you a daughter and you shall name her Mary.

" 'She shall, according to your vow, be devoted to the Lord from her infancy, and be filled with the Holy Spirit from her mother's womb. She shall neither eat nor drink anything which is unclean, nor shall her conversation be among the common people but in the Temple of the Lord.

" 'When you come to the Golden Gate of Jerusalem, you shall there meet your wife Anna. . . . '[1]

"And now I meet you here. We shall have a daughter. And she will be blessed above all women of the world."

They were full of joyful certainty, and they knew that the divine promise was going to be fulfilled.

When nine months had passed, Anna had a daughter as beautiful as the lilies of the fields, and she named her Mary.

Tradition says that Mary was the mother of all the world servers who came and dwelt in her and were born, nourished, loved, and cared for by her until they became conscious of their divine task.

In various traditions she was called by different names such as Mary, Mother of the World, Isis, Ishtar, Sophia, Kali, Lakshmi, Dakkar, and others.

> *I have already made mention about the Mother of Buddha and Christ.*
>
> *Indeed it is time to point out that the one Mother of both Lords is not a symbol but a Great Manifestation of the Feminine Origin, in which is revealed the spiritual Mother of Christ and Buddha.*
>
> *She it was Who taught and ordained Them for achievement.*[2]

When Mary was six months old, she stood, and one day she ran seven steps toward her mother's lap. When she was one year old, her father and mother took her to

---

[1] *The Lost Books of the Bible*, "The Gospel of the Birth of Mary," Chs. 1-3.
[2] Agni Yoga Press, *Leaves of Morya's Garden*, Vol. II, p. 131.

the Temple, and the Priests put their hands over her head and blessed her in great admiration for her beauty, gentleness, and grace.

When Mary was three years old, her mother and father thought that they were too old to give her the proper spiritual care, and they decided to dedicate her to the Temple. They said, "If we wait any longer she will grow up. Then it will be more difficult to make her detach herself from us, and if we have to force her to stay at the Temple, she will miss us."

So they took her to the Temple in Jerusalem. And when she saw the clean marble steps, she ran up and entered by herself into the Temple and went and embraced the high priest as though he were her father. When her mother and father came up to the hall of the priests, she danced with joy in front of them and assured them that this was what she wanted. The parents returned home in great joy, having the conviction that they had played their role in a great drama to be unveiled. This was the prelude to a greater drama.

5

▲ THE GLORIOUS SUNRISE ▲

MARY LIVED in the Temple of Jerusalem until her fourteenth year. She lived the purest life possible for a child — physically, emotionally, and mentally. Her physical environment was beautiful. Trees, flowers, and architectural masterpieces surrounded her.

Her emotional life was enriched with beautiful ceremonies, rituals, hymns, chants, colors, and by the love and care of the Temple personnel.

Her mental life merged with the great beauty of Divine Wisdom and was disciplined by meditation and contemplation in the Temple.

Mary was so pure that she was able to be in continuous communication with the angelic kingdom. She passed through all disciplines of fasting and of emotional and mental control in long years of silence, loneliness, and prayers.

In this drama you can see how the father and mother, in great aspiration, prepared themselves by fasting, meditation, and prayer in order to give birth to such an advanced soul.

Now Mary had passed many years of extreme discipline, meditation, and worship, preparing herself for a greater One to dwell within her and play a greater role in the greater drama of revelation.

Every moment there is this urge to bring into the world a chosen One. This urge becomes supreme when a woman raises herself to the Spiritual World and contacts the Soul Who is waiting to incarnate and render a great service to humanity.

In the esoteric teaching of Israel, purity of the body, emotions, and mind was emphasized to a great degree. Teachers thought that such purity could create the needed foundation to communicate with the invisible Guides of the race and be a pure channel for the divine Will.

Mary was preparing herself for a great mission. When she was fourteen years old, the High Priest announced that she and others who were of the same age must leave the Temple and go out into the world to marry.

When Mary heard this she was very upset, and she told the High Priest that she already had made a great vow not to marry but to spend her life as a servant of the Lord. The High Priest was very much impressed, but not being able to give a personal decision, he went into the Holy of Holies in the Temple to consult God.

"The virgin should be given and betrothed to one whose rod should flower, and at the end of the rod should sit a dove, symbolizing the spirit of God," a voice told him.

The High Priest called those men of the house and family of David who were marriageable. Everyone brought his rod.

There was a man called Joseph who was of a very advanced age. When his time came to pass in front of the High Priest, a dove came out of his rod and settled on its tip.

The Priest said to Joseph, "You have been chosen to take into your care the Virgin of the Lord."

Joseph took Mary, with seven other girls her age, to her mother's home in Galilee. Then he went to Bethlehem to set his house in order and make the needed preparations to receive her at his home. In cases where a man was very elderly, he would keep a young girl as his servant, caretaker, or as an adopted child.

Many months later when Joseph came to Galilee to take Mary home, he saw with great surprise that she was with child. He said, weeping, "You took the vow to remain a virgin. . . . How am I going to explain this great tragedy that you have brought upon my house, on my name and good reputation?"

Mary was extremely calm, full of peace and grace as she approached him.

"Do not worry," she said. "I never saw a man. I am still a virgin. God is Almighty, and everything is possible for Him. Is there anything that God cannot do?

"The fact is, I was at the fountain to fill my pitcher when a glorious Angel stood at my side and said, 'Mary, peace be with you. Behold, a light from heaven will come and dwell in you. The Power of the Highest will overshadow you, and you, a virgin, will conceive and bear a son.'

"I was very much afraid, but then I said, 'Let His Will be done. . . .' I am innocent, Joseph, and have known no man."

Joseph also was very much afraid and did not know what to do. After long hours of conflict within himself, at last he slept and had a dream.

The Angel of the Lord came and said, "Joseph, do not be afraid to take her under your care, for what has grown in her is from the Holy Spirit. And she will bear a son, and you will call him Jesus."

Joseph arose early in the morning and took the virgin to his home. He took care of her and kept her in chastity.

But a few weeks later, a rumor spread in Galilee, Bethlehem, and Jerusalem that Mary was with child. And one day they both were arrested by the temple guards and taken to the High Priest.

Joseph was bitterly reproached by the High Priest, but he replied, "Lord, I am innocent." He swore that he had never touched Mary.

So the High Priest asked Mary about the baby. She said, "No one has touched me!"

The High Priest and his companions were very angry. "How, then, and from where did this baby come?"

They put Mary and Joseph through a great trial which was called an "ordeal." They presented to them a cup of the Lord's water. If a man, after drinking the water, was affected by it and became sick, he was found guilty. If not, he was innocent.

Joseph was given the cup, and he remained unharmed. Then Mary drank from the cup, and she, too, was found to be innocent.

Then the High Priest said, "If the Lord God has not exposed your sins, neither do I judge you. Go in peace."

Joseph and Mary were released, and they went home rejoicing and glorifying the Lord, the Almighty One. At that time, the Emperor Augustus sent out the order to take a census of all the people in his empire. We are told that both Joseph and Mary owned dwellings in Judea. Mary had inherited them from her mother and wanted her child to be born on the premises and acknowledged as its heir. The retainers and servants in charge of this property were either Essenes or Assyrians.

On the way to Bethlehem, Mary was ready to deliver the child. Poor Joseph ran here and there to find a place, but all the houses and hotels were full because of the census. At last he found a cave at the side of a hill, which was used as a stable for animals. Then Joseph took her down off the donkey, and she had her child and put it in a manger which was full of hay.

The invisible power behind this live drama arranged it that at the same time a *solar* drama was being enacted in relation to our earth.

Thrice Greatest Hermes saw this relation between the great and the small, between above and below, and formulated his famous words, "As above, so below."

Annie Besant, one of the great disciples of Helena Petrovna Blavatsky, says,

> ... He is always born at the winter solstice, after the shortest day in the year, at the midnight of the 24th of December, when the sign Virgo is rising above the horizon; born as this sign is rising, he is born always of a virgin, and she remains virgin after she has given birth to her Sun-Child, as the celestial Virgo remains unchanged and unsullied when the Sun comes forth from her in the heavens. Weak,

feeble as an infant is he, born when the days are shortest and the nights are longest....[1]

Alice A. Bailey, the great disciple of Master K. H., says in her book *From Bethlehem to Calvary*:

> At the time of the birth of Christ, Sirius, the Star in the East, was on the meridian line, Orion, called "The Three Kings" by oriental astronomers, was in proximity; therefore the constellation Virgo, the Virgin, was rising in the east, and the line of the ecliptic, of the equator and of the horizon all met in that constellation. It is interesting also to note that the brightest and largest star in the constellation Virgo is called Spica; it is to be found in the "ear of corn" (sign of fertility) which the Virgin holds. Bethlehem means the "house of bread," and there is therefore an obvious connection between these two words. This constellation is also composed of three stars in the shape of a cup. This is the true Holy Grail, that which contains the life blood, the repository of the sacred and the holy, and that which conceals divinity.... In the sun's journey around the zodiac, this "Man of the Heavens" eventually arrives at Pisces; this sign is exactly opposite the sign Virgo, and is the sign of all world Saviours.... The age of Christianity is the Piscean age, and Christ came to the Holy Land when our sun transited into that sign. Therefore that which was started and had its being in Virgo (the birth of the Christ Child) is consummated

---

[1] Besant, Annie, *Esoteric Christianity*, 8th ed., 1966, pp. 109-110.

in Pisces when that Christ Child, having attained maturity, comes forth as the world Saviour.

... Closely associated with the constellation Virgo, and to be found in the same section of the Heavens, are three other constellations, and in these three there is portrayed for us symbolically the story of the Child which shall be born, suffer and die and come again. There is the group of stars called Coma Berenice, the Woman with the Child. There is Centaurus, the Centaur, and Boötes, whose name in the Hebrew language means the "Coming One." First, the child born of the woman and that woman a virgin; then the centaur, ever the symbol of humanity in the ancient mythologies, for man is an animal, plus a god, and therefore a human being. Then He Who shall come looms over them all, overshadowing them, pointing to the fulfillment which shall come through birth and human incarnation.[1]

Let us recall a few other names related to the story of Jesus that have symbolic meaning. For example, in Cruden's *Concordance*, Nazareth means "that which is consecrated or set apart." Galilee means "turning of the wheel." Bethlehem means "house of bread." Christ said that He was the bread of Life, and . . . "except a grain of wheat fall into the ground and die, it abideth alone: but if it die, it bringeth forth much fruit."[2]

St. Luke, in his testament, says at the time Mary gave birth to her Son:

---

[1] Bailey, Alice A., *From Bethlehem to Calvary*, pp. 63-64.
[2] John 12:24

> *There were shepherds in that region where they were staying, and they were watching their flocks at night.*
>
> *And behold, the angel of God came to them, and the glory of the Lord shone on them; and they were seized with a great fear.*
>
> *And the angel said to them, "Do not be afraid; for behold, I bring you glad tidings of great joy, which will be to all the world.*
>
> *"For this day is born to you in the city of David, a Savior . . . and this is a sign for you: You will find the babe wrapped in swaddling clothes and lying in a manger." And suddenly there appeared with the angel a heavenly host, praising God and saying,*
>
> *"Glory to God in the highest, and on earth peace and good will for men."*
>
> *. . . And they came with haste, and found Mary and Joseph, and the babe laid in a manger.*[1]

There is another beautiful story given by Master Morya about the star and about the birth of Jesus. It says:

> *What Star was it that guided the Magi? Of course it was the Command of the Brotherhood: To hail Jesus, to safeguard and bring some means to the poor family.*
>
> *We walked over the face of the earth not knowing the exact spot. The Commands of the Teraphim*

---

[1] Luke 2:8-16
NOTE: The manger was a long box, five to six feet long, two feet wide and one foot deep, in which hay or grain was placed for the animals to eat.

directed us or led us from day to day. When we heard, "It is near!," we had just lost all signs of habitation. Could one expect a miracle of so unprecedented an Annunciation in the midst of camel dung and the braying of donkeys? Human thought attempted to locate the future prophet perhaps near a temple or at least majestic walls.

We received the Command to halt at a humble inn. In the low-ceilinged house with clay walls we stopped for the night. A fire and a small oil lamp filled the room with a red glow. After our meal we noticed that a servant poured out the remains of the milk into a separate amphora. We said to her, "It is not right to save it."

"But," she said, "it is not for Thee, O Lord, but for a poor woman. Here behind the wall lives a carpenter. Recently a son was born to him."

Extinguishing the fire, we laid on our hands and asked, "Whither shall we go further?"

Came the answer, "Nearer than the nearest. Lower than the lowest. Higher than the highest." Not understanding the meaning we besought a Command, but we were told, "Let the ears harken."

And we sat in the darkness in silence. And we heard how somewhere beyond the wall a child had begun to cry. We began to mark the direction of the cry and we heard the Mother's song so often heard in the homes of husbandmen:

"Let people count thee a plower, but I know, my son, thou art a king. Who, save thee, shall raise the best seed, the most fruitful. The Lord shall call my little one and say, 'Thy seed alone hast glorified My feast. Sit with Me, king of the worthiest seeds.'"

> As we heard this song three knocks resounded in the ceiling. We said, "In the morning we shall go there."
>
> Before dawn we donned our finest garments and besought the servant to lead us in the direction of the cry.
>
> She said, "The Lord wishes to visit the family of the carpenter. I had better lead you around for here one must pass through the cattle fold."
>
> Recalling the Command, we chose the shortest way.
>
> Here behind the manger was a tiny dwelling leaning against rock. Here by the hearth was a woman and in her arms — He. What signs accompanied? He stretched out His little hand and on the palm was a red sign. Upon this sign we placed the most precious pearl of those we brought.
>
> Bestowing the treasures and the sacred objects, we warned the mother of the need of wanderings and at once we turned back crossing the same manger.
>
> Behind us the mother said, "See, my little one, thou art the king. Set this diamond upon the forehead of thy steed."
>
> We departed bearing in mind the sign of the red star upon the palm. Then, also, had been said, "Remember the day of the red star upon the forehead of the warrior."[1]

Isn't it wonderful to put together the pieces of the jigsaw puzzle and see at least a part of that picture complete! Isn't it wonderful to think that on the night of the

---

[1] Roerich, Helena, *On Eastern Crossroads*, pp. 37-40.

Birth, Mary was coming from Jerusalem to Bethlehem, the sign Virgo was starting to rise on the horizon, Sirius was on the meridian line, and the three Kings were on their way to greet the Babe!

As the Child was taking birth, the Sun began to come out of Virgo, and when Jesus was born, the three kings that were in the heavens — the sign Orion — were greeting the rising Sun.

So these wise Ones came and presented their gifts: the first gift of gold, the second of frankincense, the third gift of myrrh. These were the symbols of the three powers that were focusing themselves upon this great Revelation: the power of Will, the power of Love, and the power of Light.

Also, humanly, they were symbolizing the threefold vehicle of man — physical, emotional, and mental — from the three kingdoms — mineral, vegetable, and animal — which were coming to offer themselves for the new revelation. And the guiding star was leading them to the cave.

The cave symbolizes the shortest day and the last point of materialization from which starts the path of spiritualization, the path of conscious evolution. As the sun would grow in light, so the Son would grow in wisdom and influence, until the height of midday.

At Christmas time we decorate our trees, which is a very old custom, because the tree was also one of the factors in the great drama since the foundation of the Hierarchy.

Christ said that He was the tree and we were the branches. He wanted us to be live branches, bringing forth the fruit of our good deeds. We decorate our Christmas trees with candles or lights, symbolizing the deepest aspiration of our hearts. This aspiration is that we should be a green tree, a tree with lights blooming forth and with gifts piled all around our trunk.

The lights symbolize our subtle centers which number seventy-seven. In a perfect man all these centers must open, unfold, and radiate their colorful, divine hues, like palpitating hearts, with their proper virtues and energies. As the tree shines forth with lights, we say that the Christ-consciousness within man increases and eventually becomes "a light in the world."

The gifts at the foot of the tree suggest what only a blooming man can give. He has the abundance of life, and he gives life to whatever he touches. He gives mentally, emotionally, and physically and dedicates what he gives to the service of the growing light within.

In the story of the Star, we are told that the three Magi dressed in their best garments before meeting the Child. This is very significant. In mystical language the garments are the vehicles of man. They must be purified, made beautiful, and then the human entity within them becomes able to approach higher levels of consciousness, the higher worlds, and puts to use the growing light within.

6

▲ The Three Magi or the Kings ▲

Tradition says there were three great Initiates who were sent by the Hierarchy to go and help the Child financially and spiritually. The *New Testament* does not give much information about them. The fact is, they not only gave the needed financial help to make a decent life for Mary and Joseph and for raising the Child, but also they gave esoteric instructions to the parents on how to guide the Child as He grew, how to protect Him from various dangers, and what Plan was unfolding behind all these events.

Mary was aware of many things that were to come, but her consciousness, so to say, was focused upon the day when she would know fully the meaning and purpose of all that was happening.

The names of the Magi were Melchior, Caspar, and Balthazar. They were Initiate Disciples in contact with the Hierarchy, and they were serving as three kings of different countries in the East.

Melchior was the son of an Arab king living in Petra, where there was a little center for the Hierarchical Teaching and the lesser mysteries. He brought frankincense which was abundant in the area and used for temple ceremonies and rituals.

Caspar was an Initiate living in Persia and India, and it was he who brought gold because he was very rich.

Balthazar was an olden Egyptian and Ethiopian Initiate. His name is mentioned in Ethiopian history as Bees Bazen, about whom it was said: "In the year eight of the reign of Bazen, Christ was born."

The myrrh which he brought was found mostly in the Red Sea area inhabited by Ethiopians and Egyptians.

We are told that one of the Magi was carrying a Teraphim. This was a little wooden picture which was highly magnetized by Great Ones and given to the Initiates as a magnetic link between the Hierarchy and the Initiates, a kind of communication line, similar to our walkie-talkie, which would lead them to the right destination.

The Magi were very advanced astrologers and were individually called *Magus* which means Master. The interesting point is that in all ages such advanced beings visited a great Soul when He was incarnated. For example, at the birth of Krishna, the Star was seen and Great Ones visited Him. A similar story is told of Buddha's birth, of Confucius' birth, and also the same stories are told about the births of Mithra, Socrates, Asclepius, Romulus, Bacchus, Zoroaster, Hermes, and others.

In some esoteric writings we are told that after the three Magi met the Mother, Joseph, and the Child, and after they gave their instructions and the greetings of the

Great Brotherhood, they went to Mount Carmel where there was an esoteric center. There they recorded the event, left instructions for the future of the Child, and then went on to Egypt. Many, many times they came in contact with Jesus, leading Him until He reached the age of thirty.

7

▲ Preparation ▲

Preparation of the vehicles is very important for the coming child.

People prepare clothes for the child. They make ready those things that are going to be used for him. But only a very few mothers prepare themselves — emotionally, mentally, and spiritually — to attract and nourish an advanced, coming soul.

In addition to physical health, emotional, mental, and spiritual health is important to the mother who wants to give birth to Souls who will lead humanity on the Path of discipleship and initiation.

In esoteric literature we are told that both father and mother must consecrate themselves before any relationship starts. This consecration should be done by being careful of what one eats and drinks. For example, no wine, no alcohol, no drugs, no tobacco must be used by a woman who is going to conceive or is pregnant. This will help the coming child not only physically but also will provide a strong foundation for his emotional, mental, and spiritual life.

We are told that the pregnant woman must have a serene emotional life surrounded by the beauty of Nature, the beauty of the written and spoken word, by music, or any other of the arts that uplifts her into the world of harmony, rhythm, color, sound, and motion. She should meditate daily on lofty thoughts; feed her imagination with great images, heroes, and leaders of all ages; and always be full of compassion, forgiveness, and serenity. Only to such women are great sons and daughters born who carry on their lives in great success and beauty.

In the future there will be special colleges where girls and women will learn how to conceive greater souls, how to evoke the greatest potential within these souls while yet unborn, how to raise them with the greatest understanding and thus give to the future a solid beauty of mind, emotions, and body. Many books have been written on this subject, but it is not the books nor the lectures that will help. Instead, a practical life of meditation and the proper environment will help mothers achieve their visions. In the future there will be outlined special plans for discipline, dedication, and purification before women decide to have a child.

Mary was in the right place and under the best influences to enable her to carry out her sacred mission in preparing the body of a great Initiate.

We are told that there are three openings in the human aura through which a soul can depart or enter and possess his vehicle.

One is the solar plexus, through which most children enter into the physical plane. These are the average citizens who can either improve themselves through education and discipline or live a life of slavery.

The second door is the etheric heart center. Some humanitarian and philanthropically oriented people come to the physical plane via this center. They have a more advanced heart and some sense of responsibility and unity.

Those who come via the head center are those who are truly advanced in service, sacrifice, and intellect.

This is why in olden times people were trained to unfold and open their higher gate to welcome greater ones into the world. The stage of unfoldment of these centers depends on the life that the mother and father are living. The condition of the centers of both parents must be taken into consideration, and the time of preparation for parenthood must be dedicated to unselfish service and meditation so that higher centers will be activated and unfold.

To bring a child into the world in the past was based on personal joy and family and national interests. In the future, women will bring children into this life only for the purpose of serving humanity. Mothers must be thoroughly informed on how to raise their children so that they will further the progress of humanity in all fields and on all levels. Motherhood will take on a more serious and deeper meaning. The greatest responsibility of a mother will be in helping her child bloom into greater beauty.

The Virgin Mary stands as an indication of ideal motherhood.

Sleep, rest, absence of nervous tension and irritation, the right food and drink, and the right relationship with people who are full of loving care — such should be the atmosphere surrounding a pregnant woman. In the advanced schools of the esoteric Path, the most important factor was the purification and discipline of the mind which was achieved through concentration, meditation, and contemplation.[1]

Concentration was taught through physical exercises, games, and physical plane service. For example, a student of Wisdom should clean his rooms or work in the garden and do these things with real interest and in a state of mind control. A student should be taught how to knit, how to use hammer and saw, and how to weave. Most handicrafts were taught in these schools. Jewelry making, carpentry, blacksmithing, masonry, and other crafts were used to develop concentration and alignment between body, emotions, and mind. The motto was: "Labor with your whole attention, interest, and joy." Thus the student learned control over his vehicles through concentration.

The Bhagavad Gita says that "concentration is yoga" because in concentration we create unity and integration within the threefold personality.

Meditation was taught by taking a verse from the Ageless Wisdom and thinking about it for a certain time daily.

Contemplation is meditation of a higher degree, and it was used by advanced students and servers. Contemplation is an act of Soul-infusion in which the fountain of joy and the blueprints of the Plan are touched. This was accomplished by advanced occult meditation after building the Rainbow Bridge through which the focus of consciousness is withdrawn from the lower

---

[1] Saraydarian, Torkom, *The Science of Meditation*, Chs. VI-XXII.

mental planes and fused with the energy field of the Chalice and the Soul. Thus, the disciple learned the technique of coming in contact with divine ideas, as ideas are fractions of the great, dynamic, electrical Plan which the Hierarchy forms in translating the Purpose of the Logos.[1]

In sacred schools or communities children were accepted as the gifts of God, and parents tried to bring the best out of their being. In old traditions the pregnant woman was sacred. She was considered a holy temple through whom a part of God was incarnating. This temple should be filled with lofty ideas, ecstasy, and radioactive love. All these will create the right atmosphere for the mother, and through this energy field greater light will reach the baby who will grow in serenity, in peace, and in joy, blooming in all his beauty. If the atmosphere or the outer and inner condition of the mother-to-be is not pure and she is not in communication with the higher worlds but is occupied with negative emotions and distorted thoughts, she will attract undeveloped ones who karmically will find the right mother through whom to be born and become conditioned by all the glamors, illusions, and distorted ideas of their mother. But sometimes it happens that, for karmic reasons, beautiful souls are caught in the net, and, because of a lack of a proper atmosphere, their evolution is hindered and their future life becomes complicated.

This is also true of an incarnating idea. If our mental, emotional, and etheric fields are not clean, harmonious,

---

[1] See *The Science of Becoming Oneself* by Torkom Saraydarian, Ch. XVIII.

and rhythmic, great ideas which may reach us will turn into glamors, illusions, and maya and will serve only our personal and separative urges and vanities. Under such conditions man becomes a destructive agent.

It is not only imperative that the child have the right psychological atmosphere in the womb, but after he is born he must have an atmosphere of love, understanding, and beauty in his home. Sometimes a child has both of these factors, but there must also be added the right atmosphere in the community until the child is at least fourteen. For this reason, in ancient Israel, Egypt, and India, people had many kinds of communes where the child, as a gift of God, could grow in an atmosphere of spiritualized relationship and bloom to his fullest capacity. A good child can be spoiled if he is not placed in the right environment and atmosphere.

In some parts of Asia the pregnant woman was kept away from those people who were negatively oriented, morally low, gossipy, and full of ill-will. It was believed that contact with such people might pollute the atmosphere of the growing embryo and have a bad effect on the child. A pregnant woman was kept away from loud parties, heavy work, and alcohol and kept busy with Nature, religious services, lofty literature, and music. She was given the opportunity to sleep well and to keep company only with those who were happy, healthy, and full of love and wisdom. It was believed that such a condition would help the future child greatly.

If we compare this situation with the present age, we find the reason why we have so many problems with delinquency. Today's pregnant women drive their cars every day in tension and fear. They work under manifold pressures and many kinds of irritation. They spend many hours watching television through which crime, greed, hatred, jealousy, and fear are continuously being impressed on the consciousness of the growing entity. Add to this the pollution of water, food, and air. Such an atmosphere will not be beneficial to the coming baby, and after he is born he still does not have ideal conditions. Mother soon must return to work. The baby sitter will take her place, and eventually the child will be exposed to the television with all its evil influence. He will usually be left alone until the father and mother return home, and the love they will show him will not be full of energy and radiation. Under these conditions the child will not have the necessary attention, care, and companionship of his mother especially and very little from his father.

The conception, growth, birth, and expansion of a great idea need the same proper conditions as an incarnating soul. A great idea needs the right mental, emotional, etheric, and physical conditions to be conceived in its full beauty and be expressed in its totality without being twisted, distorted, and polluted through a mental, emotional, and etheric atmosphere in which there exist heavy layers of illusions, dark clouds of glamor, and crystallizations. Such an atmosphere cannot be conducive to great inspirations, ideas, and visions but serves only for the distortion and degeneration of ideas.

As in chemistry, the mixture of diverse elements produces different results. We know that our mental, emotional, and etheric bodies are substantial. These substances produce different results when they come in contact with various kinds of energies or forces, and these forces or energies produce disparate results as they pass through different conditions of the subtle vehicles of the human being.

Each thought, each idea, and each vision is the result of the combination of the incoming energy and the vehicles on which the energy is impressed. That is why the inner chemistry is another occult subject for careful research and study.

To further the evolution of a nation, the most intensive care must be given to mothers and to the teachers under whom children will grow and learn about life. Until we change our homes and schools, we cannot change the nation.

8

▲ Through Many Lands ▲

WHEN JESUS was two years old, His parents took Him to Egypt at the order of a great Messenger. There were two reasons behind this act.

1. Herod, knowing that a great King was born who could be the future leader of the people, wanted to kill Him. Because he could not find this expected leader, Herod ordered his soldiers to kill all male children in that area under two years of age, thinking that in this way he might kill Jesus.

2. They went to Egypt for special instruction in the Egyptian mysteries. They were told to go to Egypt and meet certain Great Ones there to learn about Jesus. Jesus was a high degree Initiate in a baby's body Who needed a great deal of protection, physically and mentally.

It would not be easy to raise Him, and the parents needed instruction on how to feed Him and how to handle Him so that He would be able, in the future, to perform His most difficult part of a divine drama in accordance with the Plan of the Hierarchy. They went to special classes in the Egyptian mysteries where they learned about the past of Jesus and His future activities. Also, they highly disciplined their own vehicles.

They learned about His relationship with the Hierarchy of the Masters and Angels. The most important instruction they received was on how to protect Jesus physically, emotionally, and mentally so that no wrong was done to Him. Otherwise, there could be fatal damage to the highly sensitive bodies of Jesus, rendering Him unable to perform His great labor.

He was given to His parents as a great treasure to care for, and it was necessary that they should know what to do under many circumstances. If they were kept ignorant of the whole drama, they could create many obstacles and distortions. They would need to perform their part very accurately in order to help Jesus perform His part. Actually, they were going to Egypt on a secret mission which was revealed only to a limited number of Initiates who left few records about this mission.

The family spent three years in Egypt where Jesus enjoyed the great temples, the aura of great Masters, and was flooded with Their blessings. When the instruction of the parents was complete, they returned to Palestine and Jesus entered the mystery school on Mount Carmel.

At that time there were five great centers and their many groups in Asia and Greece, all forming a five-pointed star of great Revelation.

One was in Armenia near Mount Ararat upon which Noah's Ark had rested.

Another one was in Palestine on Mount Carmel, the community of which was situated on the northern shore of the Dead Sea. This was known as the Essene community.

The third was in Egypt, the fourth was in Greece, and the fifth was between Chaldea and Persia. These centers were intended to prepare leaders to enlighten humanity about the "kingdom of God" and the hierarchical Plan.

The Armenian school dealt mostly with Cosmic rays and, curiously enough, today Armenians have a mountain on which is located a very advanced observatory which deals mainly with Cosmic rays. The leader of the observatory is a well-know scientist and the president of the World Astronomical Society.

The center in Palestine was mostly dedicated to religious mysteries, worship, and sacraments. The Essene community exercised and put into practice the Teaching of this center.

The Essene community was a secondary school, a branch led by the center on Mount Carmel. Many races were represented there. The community was situated at the northern shore of the Dead Sea. The Essenes, who were very learned people, were visited by advanced Masters from Egypt, Armenia, Persia, and Greece.

In Egypt the center was an advanced one based on the science of communication with the higher worlds: the esoteric secrets of astronomy, chemistry, sound, and architecture. The secrets of how to detach the real man from the body, from the emotional and lower mental worlds, and how to put him in contact with the world of archetypes were known to the ancients.

In Greece the center or college dealt mainly with the development and integration of the higher mind, logic, reason, and pure Intuition and the expression of creative beauty in the fields of poetry, oratory, dance, and music.

In Chaldea and Persia the focus was on magic and the use of the mind upon matter through the manipulation of the fires of the Universe in man.

The heads of these five schools were Initiates. They had been informed by the Hierarchy of the important event in which Jesus was to play the great role.

The Essenes were primarily healers. They celebrated the sacraments of Baptism and Holy Communion,[1] two of the most important sacraments of the church which were taken from the Essenes.

Baptism was a sacrament to purify the emotional responses of a human being. This was not a ritual but a scientific procedure. First, the water was magnetized by chants and prayers, charging it with high-voltage energy from the Intuitional Plane. Next, the would-be disciple was submerged in the water to be purified from any uncleanliness which hung on his astral body, either from former lives or from his parents or associates. The neophyte received great emotional release, purification, and protection by Baptism.

Baptism would take place either seven, twelve, or thirty years after the neophyte was initiated into the mystery school or into the Brotherhood.

---

[1] These and other sacraments were taught in all these centers of learning in the world by great Masters many thousands of years before the Christian era.

Holy Communion was celebrated in the form of a supper where bread and wine were blessed and shared by all present. This was the Sacrament of Brotherhood and communicants vowed to stand together in the service of a great idea.

When a neophyte had spent five years in the Brotherhood, he was represented as a five-year-old child; when he had passed twelve years there, he was a mature man; after thirty years he was a perfected one.

According to tradition, Jesus began to teach when He was fifty-four years old. He was baptized on His birthday when He was "thirty years old" and started His great mission.

In their Teachings, the Essenes stressed the idea that no man should be a slave. This was of great importance and meant not only physical slavery — being dominated by others — but also that no man should be a slave to his physical urges or his emotional and mental drives and must stand in his own spiritual light as a free observer and actor. This was the meaning of self-actualization taught by the Essenes in their communal life. They also anticipated the coming Teacher of Righteousness Who would eliminate war, because war was an action resulting from slavery both in its outer and esoteric meaning. A wise man once said, "Every virtuous man is free."

Future revelations will show that the five great centers of learning referred to were connected with each other in spiritual communication, and all their Teachings were organized by an esoteric purpose, upon a common plan. They all formed parts of a great picture.

The existence of these centers of learning is cyclical. The Teachers appear for certain times, perform their duties, and withdraw. When the real Teachers withdraw at the command of the Hierarchy, their followers continue for a while, imitating their Teachers. This eventually leads to degeneration, distortion, and confusion within the centers themselves.

It is within such a state of disintegration that a new shoot comes out which synthesizes in itself the essence of the past and the vision of the future. The shoot grows, having its roots within the essence of the centers, and causes further disintegration within the form side of the centers until they disappear. It takes centuries for this shoot to grow and form new centers of revelation, once more at the appropriate locations. This process of the formation of centers, their degeneration, and the coming of a new Prophet of Light repeats itself age after age as a cyclic drama to help humanity and to initiate those who are ready to enter into the mysteries of "becoming oneself."

Jesus remained in the Essene Brotherhood until He was twelve years old. We are told that He passed a great test in the Temple of Jerusalem when Elders met Him with various questions, and at the end they expressed their great admiration.

These twelve years mean many things. He might have been actually twelve years of age, or He might have been older if we take into consideration that He spent twelve years with the Secret Brotherhood.

At the time of the examination, two of the Great Ones who had visited Him at His birth came to the Essene Brotherhood and told Him to prepare to go to India. Jesus remained seven days with His parents until the Great Ones were ready to leave. They journeyed over land for one year during which Jesus saw many lands and many different kinds of people. He saw the great darkness and suffering of the people, and the compassion in His heart deepened.

At the end of the year They reached Jagannath (Puri) where Jesus entered an advanced school of pure Buddhism taught by great Masters. It was in India that He gathered both His recorded and unrecorded parables.

From the Essenes He had learned the mysteries of the emotional body and the astral plane. In India He learned the mysteries of the mental body and the mental plane. He completely dominated His mind and learned to function at will in His higher mind. This made Him a great white magician. Actually, magic means to have a high voltage of willpower and to use this power through the mind to control matter and energy.

Jesus arrived at the Ganges and lived in Benares for a few years. He studied and mastered the science of spiritual healing in the monastery of Jagannath under the great healer, Udraka. He stayed in the monastery of Jagannath for three years and then entered into the heart of Tibet — Lhasa.

Nicholas Roerich, who visited India and Tibet and recorded some interesting traditions, says,

> *In Shrinagar we first encountered the curious legend about Christ's [Jesus'] visit at this place. Afterwards, we saw how widely spread in India, in Ladak and in Central Asia was the Legend of the visit of the Christ to these parts during his long absence quoted in the Gospel.*[1]

---

[1] Roerich, Nicholas, *Heart of Asia*, p. 23.

> *In Leh, we again encountered the legend of Christ's visit to these parts. They told us that . . . not far from the bazaar there still exists a pond, near which stood an old tree. Under this tree, Christ preached to the people before His departure to Palestine. We also heard another legend of how Christ, when young, arrived in India with a merchant's caravan, and how He continued to study the higher wisdom in the Himalayas.*[1]

It was in the Himalayas that Jesus met Great Ones Who unveiled to Him the part He was to play in the forthcoming great drama. Here, for the first time, He realized the great responsibility which was descending on His shoulders.

After Jesus left the Himalayas, He visited one of the Magi who had come to see Him. At that time He was living in a monastery in Persia. Here He perfected His healing powers and methods; He studied the mystery of silence; He learned how to silence His nature by holding His vibration in such high frequency that it could create an electrical wall and prevent any unwanted impression from reaching His mechanism. After building this wall of silence, He could enter into communication with the Great Ones and carry Their message to the world. All great missions are performed after a long period of silence and loneliness. Jesus referred to such a silence when He said, "But you, when you pray, enter into your inner chamber and lock your door, and pray to your Fa-

---

[1] Roerich, Nicholas, *Heart of Asia*, p. 29.

ther Who is in secret, and your Father who sees in secret He Himself shall reward you openly."[1]

After spending more than a year in Persia, Jesus went to Chaldea to study the esoteric sense of timing and the mysteries of the stars. On leaving Chaldea He visited Greece where He took part in the Dionysian mysteries and studied in various temples. It was in Greece that great Egyptian Masters met Him and invited Him to come to Egypt to receive His final instructions before starting His world mission in Palestine.

During this time those who were going to play a part in the divine drama in Palestine were being gathered together by an invisible Hand. At that time there were forty Great Masters in Egypt. Jesus lived there until He was "twenty-nine years old." He passed three important tests in Egypt before He went to Palestine. These were tests of

Sincerity

Justice

Faith

Sincerity was proof that He had been a Third Degree Initiate in a past life — proof that once upon a time He had stood before His own Divine Self and had seen the vision of His essence, proof that He had stood before the Ancient of Days and was enlightened. Justice proved that He had no evil karma to pay. He was pure and innocent. Faith proved that He would never forsake His mission; despite adverse conditions He would play His part in the great Drama of Revelation.

---

[1] Matthew 6:6

The Egyptian Masters gave Him the name "The Sun of Righteousness."[1] According to esoteric books, initiates repeat on higher spirals each initiation through which they pass before proceeding to the next one. In Egypt Jesus culminated His past achievement and was ready to start His great mission in Palestine.

---

[1] H.P. Blavatsky says in *Isis Unveiled*, Vol. II, p. 386, "The child born was Jesus, named Joshua. Adopted by his uncle Rabbi Jehosuah, he was initiated into the secret doctrine by Rabbi Elhanan, a kabalist, and then by the Egyptian priests, who consecrated him High Pontiff of the Universal Secret Doctrine, on account of his great mystic qualities."

9

▲ In the Past ▲

THOSE WHO fail to make the grade at the close of each solar system are held in pralaya to have another chance when the next solar system is formed. They incarnate in the proper chain and on the proper globe to carry on their evolution.[1]

According to the esoteric Teaching, there was a group of people held in pralaya between the first and second solar systems. These people came into incarnation in the early Lemurian times, when our earth humanity was not yet individualized. They were more advanced than our earth humanity, and, because of that, they held leading positions in all human affairs.

We are told that in the late Lemurian times a group of very advanced disciples of this race stood at the portal of initiation. Most of them passed, but three great disciples failed to pass the door because of their love of riches and

---

[1] Read about the formation of solar systems and about chains and globes in *Cosmos in Man* by Torkom Saraydarian.

material possessions. These three disciples, being rejected for initiation, committed a crime. They slew their own Master Builder Who could open the door for them into higher evolution and give them the word to enable them to enter.

After the murder they were horrified by what they had done and desperately searched for forgiveness and light. It was their search that produced the first Masonic tradition as a process of symbols and rituals to enter the door of Initiation and find the Lost Word, which is the innermost Self of every man.

The ancient records say that, years later, the three disciples were put to death. This was a symbolic death as these three disciples represent the lower man, the personality, which must be "lost" to reveal the Real Self, the Word Incarnate.

Tradition says that Jesus of Nazareth was a direct descendant of the eldest of these three disciples. Jesus very successfully walked the path of enlightenment, and He reversed the path leading to materialism and possessions.

There is no doubt in my mind that the rich man who stood in front of Jesus was one of the followers of the original disciples. To this rich man, Jesus suggested the same agelong requirement to enter the Door of Initiation. He said, "Leave everything behind you and follow Me. . . ."

▲

Every man is primarily the result of his past, and Jesus was no exception. Christian mystics, in the fire of their fanaticism, changed the real man — Jesus, the son of man — into a myth, a god who incarnated in the form of a man.

It is both encouraging and interesting to know that He was a man, like you and me, Who worked very hard and accomplished much on the path of perfection through continuous striving, sacrifice, and service. This is why He had an understanding heart and a great divine compassion. This does not deny that He is of divine origin. Everyone in the Universe is created by the Great Life and lives, moves, and breathes within Him as one of His Sparks. Jesus always emphasized this, as when He said: "I am the Son of man." "I go to my Father and to your Father." "Greater things will you do." By such expressions Jesus revealed His true manhood and opened the path to divinity. To know that He is a man Who has reached such heights of achievement is the greatest inspiration for a human being. What He did as a man, we can do! But if what He did was done as a God, how can we do what He did?

The Tibetan Master gives us some clues to His past lives when he says that Jesus was ". . . Joshua the Son of Nun, appearing again in the time of Ezra as Jeshua, taking the third initiation, as related in the book of Zechariah, as Joshua."[1] Joshua was the minister of Moses, and it was He who followed Moses when he ascended Mount Sinai.[2] It was upon Joshua the Lord wanted Moses to put his hand. Also, the Lord told Moses to "make him to stand before Eleazar the priest and before all the congregation; and put him in charge in

---

[1] Bailey, Alice A., *Initiation Human and Solar*, p. 56.
[2] See Exodus 24:13.

their sight."¹ We are told that "Joshua the son of Nun [fish] was full of the spirit of wisdom; for Moses had laid his hands upon him; and the children of Israel obeyed him, and did as the Lord commanded Moses."² It was Joshua who commanded the armies of Israel in their first battle shortly after they left Egypt. Born in Egypt He was of the tribe of Ephraim.

After Moses had departed the Lord said to Joshua, ". . . arise, cross this Jordan, you and all this people, into the land which I am giving to them . . . ."³ He was a second degree initiate who was able to "cross" the river Jordan and lead His people into the promised land through a process of purification and control of the emotional nature. After crossing the river Jordan, at the command of the Lord, Joshua organized the people and the priests to encircle the tall walls of Jericho once a day for six days and seven times on the seventh day. "And on the seventh day, they rose in the morning, and compassed the city after the same manner seven times; it was on that day only that they compassed the city seven times. At the seventh time, when the priests blew the trumpets, Joshua said to the people, Shout; for the Lord has delivered the city to you . . . and the wall fell down flat, so that the people went up into the city . . . and they took the city."⁴

A very interesting event is related concerning the victory at Jericho. Before conquering it, Joshua sent two spies to the city where they entered into the house of a

---

[1] Numbers 27:19
[2] Deuteronomy 34:9
[3] Joshua 1:1-2
[4] Joshua 6:15-20

harlot, Rahab. The king of Jericho sought to kill them, but "the woman took the two men, and hid them and said, 'Truly, the men came to me, but I did not know where they came from.' " She had taken them up to the roof of the house and hidden them beneath stalks of flax which she had piled there. The men were saved, went back, and reported to Joshua. After the fall of Jericho, Joshua spared the life of this harlot and her family. Tradition says that it was she who poured the expensive oil upon the feet of Jesus and wrapped them with her hair.

Joshua was a mighty warrior, and His wisdom and power were from the Lord. We are told that He entered with His people into the promised land which He divided among the twelve tribes of Israel. He dwelt in a city called Timnath-serah, which means the fruitful portion, and at the age of one hundred and ten He passed away and was buried there on Mount Ephraim. This mighty warrior, because of the love of His people and because of His great closeness to the Lord, came once more to the people of Israel in the name of Jeshua (or Joshua), the High Priest. This time He was a warrior in the spiritual realm, rendering a great service on higher planes as a High Priest. The prophet Zechariah gives a description of a mysterious ceremony which clearly indicated that Joshua took the Initiation of Enlightenment or Transfiguration. He writes:

> *Then he showed me Joshua the high priest standing before the angel of the Lord, and Satan standing at his right hand to harm him. And the angel of the Lord said to Satan, "The Lord rebuke you, O Satan; even the Lord who has chosen*

Jerusalem rebuke you. Is not this a brand plucked out of the fire." Now Joshua was clothed with filthy garments, and stood before the angel of the Lord. And the angel answered and spoke to those who stood before him, saying, "Take away the filthy garments from him." And to him he said, "Behold, I have caused your iniquity to pass from you, and I will clothe you with good raiment." And he said, "Let them put a clean mitre on his head and clothe him with good garments." ... And the angel of the Lord charged Joshua, saying, "Thus says the Lord of Hosts: If you will walk in my ways and keep my commandments, then you shall also judge my house and keep my courts, and I will grant you to walk among these that stand by. Hear now, O Joshua the high priest, you and your fellows who stand before you; for you are marvelous men: Behold, I will bring forth the rising of the sun upon my servant. For behold the stone that I have laid before Joshua; upon one stone shall be seven facets; behold, I will open its gates, says the Lord of hosts, and I will remove the iniquity of that land in that day. In that day, says the Lord of hosts, every man shall invite his neighbor under the vine and under the fig tree." [1]

We can see that Joshua's physical, emotional, and mental bodies were purified, and He received the garment of glory and beauty. These refer to the Transfiguration Initiation. Only a transfigured man has the right to

---

[1] Zechariah 3:1-14

present himself as the High Priest and have direct communication with the Almighty One.

At the Third Initiation the personality is related to the Inner God, and thus it is flooded with the greater light. The Third Initiation is the initiation in which the Dweller on the Threshold is completely destroyed. In the above quotation it is symbolized by Satan. The Dweller on the Threshold is the sum total of physical, emotional, and mental obstacles on the path, thus blocking the path toward the goal of the disciple. At this stage the Initiate-to-be is standing in front of the Angel, but the Dweller on the Threshold, Satan, is there also, standing at his right. This means that Satan is very active, but the Solar Angel rebukes him, which means obliterates his power, and the Initiate stands only in the presence of the Angel. It is in this initiation that the personality is completely purified and passes into the glory of the Spiritual Triad, the Angel gaining full communication with the unfolding human soul, the Initiate. At that time — between 500-525 B.C. — a third degree Initiate was a great Master Who had the right to enter into the House of God, into the Hierarchy, and walk in the presence of the Great Ones.

The rising sun referred to by Zechariah means the unfolding human soul, from the core of which flashes out the monadic radiance.[1] The stone referred to means the six permanent atoms and the real Spark which forms the seventh. It is on the seventh atom that the seven gates open which lead the Initiate to the seven paths of higher evolution. Only such an Initiate will be able to invite His

---

[1] See *The Science of Meditation* by Torkom Saraydarian, pp. 54-55.

friends under "the vine tree and fig tree," which symbolize the incoming, manifesting, divine Life.

Further in the same book the great prophet Zechariah writes:

> *And the word of the Lord came to me, saying, "... make a crown and set it upon the head of Joshua ... and say to him, 'Thus says the Lord of hosts: Behold, the man whose name is Sunrise shall rise up out of his place, and he shall build the temple of the Lord.'"* [1]

The crown is the symbol of victory — victory over the personality — and entrance into the light of the Soul, the promised land, the goal. We see all this as a live drama which is carried out on two levels. One level is what is actually taking place and the other level is subjective and symbolic, to be actualized in the future.

This refers to a great disciple who is going to conquer the "promised land" within himself. He is going to build the Temple there, the Inner Temple within him, the Temple in Jerusalem, and the Lotus Temple within the higher mind where the Great One would dwell.[2]

We see now how an Initiate starts to lead a nation to prepare the great drama of salvation and revelation which was going to be unfolded in the promised land *itself.*

Initiations have two points, a starting and an ending point. The ending point is the crown of achievement, the graduation. Here Jesus started or entered into the path of the Third Initiation. He culminated it at His Trans-

---

[1] Zechariah 6:9-12
[2] See *The Science of Becoming Oneself* by Torkom Saraydarian, Ch. XII.

figuration as recorded in the *New Testament*. The starting point is the inner response to the higher Call; the ending point is the presentation of the harvest of the age-long service to the Lord of the World.

Centuries later the same individual again came to His people, this time to Aryan parents by the law of karma. John, the Beloved Disciple, tells us that He came to His own people, but they rejected Him because this time He was coming on a universal mission rather that a national one.

10

▲ THE CHRIST ▲

What is now called the Christian religion has existed among the ancients and was never absent from the beginning of the human race until Christ came in the flesh. From that time on the true *religion, which was already in existence, began to be called Christianity.*[1]

The Tibetan Sage, Master Djwhal Khul, says that "... the first human being out of that 'centre which we call the race of men' to achieve this point [the Third Initiation] was the Christ; in that first great demonstration of His point of attainment ... the Christ was joined by the Buddha. The Buddha had attained this same point prior to the creation of our planetary life, but conditions for taking the third initiation were not then available, and He and the Christ took the initiation together."[2]

---

[1] St. Augustine.
[2] Bailey, Alice A., *The Rays and the Initiations*, pp. 385-386.

Christ was called the Bodhisattva or Maitreya. Mohammedans called Him Iman Mahdi. He took His second initiation and gave the most beautiful Teaching under the name of Krishna. When you study the *New Testament* and *The Bhagavad Gita*, you will find that the same spirit radiates through them, spreading the same Teaching of the Ageless Wisdom. When Christ took the Initiation of Enlightenment, or Transfiguration, He became the Leader of the Hierarchy under the guiding eyes of that Great Being Who is mentioned in the *Bible* as the Ancient of Days, Melchizedek, or in Hindu writings as Sanat Kumara. This occurred about 600 B.C. At that time a third degree Initiate could occupy that exalted position, but in this age we are told that only a seventh degree Initiate may hold it. We are told that Buddha and Christ were completing each other to manifest the fullness of LOVE. Buddha had achieved the wisdom aspect of Love, and Christ was working to give "shape and substance to love." Eventually in Palestine Christ achieved this goal and became the embodiment of Love-Wisdom and of the Cosmic Principle of Love. Because of His achievement in the past as a human being, He "opened the door of the Third Initiation" for humanity, and a great light began to penetrate the planet. As the sons of men change into the sons of light, the light increases, and the increasing light opens gates for the striving souls to enter into a still greater light.

In religious and esoteric literature the word *Christ* has five different meanings:

▲ THE CHRIST ▲ 85

1. the inner Christ, "The Hope of Glory" or the mystical Christ[1]
2. the historical Christ
3. the Cosmic or mystic Christ
4. the Christ, the Head of the Hierarchy
5. the Archetypal Man

1. **The inner Christ** basically refers to the human soul, which is the hope of glory as it unfolds and blooms throughout ages by means of meditation, service, and sacrifice. The human soul, initiation after initiation, achieves a glorious state of awareness and radiation and becomes a savior for the lives around him. This is what Christ meant when He said that we must "be perfect as our Father in heaven," Who is the glory itself.

2. **The historical Christ** actually lived and suffered as a man, strove to surpass human limitations, and entered into a higher level of evolution. Thus He related Humanity to the Father's Home and set an example for us to follow.

3. **The Cosmic Christ** is the Soul of the Universe, the link or the relation between matter and spirit, and the redemptive energy which leads the life, sleeping in matter, toward glorious heights of endless unfoldment. In religions this is called the second person of the Trinity, the Son, the second Logos, the Love, "who is the attractive coherent force and consciousness holding all things together, who drives all mani-

---

[1] The term "Christ within," when used as a mediator, refers to the Solar Angel.

fested life toward an eventual perfection revealing the Father Aspect."

"Thus the revelation of the Son of God and the liberation of Spirit from the limitation of matter and of form is the goal. This is the Cosmic Plan. This is the macrocosm, or the God in Nature."[1] The resurrection from among the dead, or the liberation of man from life in the flesh or from the three worlds of daily living — physical, emotional, and mental — is the microcosm, or God in Man.[2] Realizing this, our individual work would appear to be:

a) to bring to the surface of our lives the revelation of the glory of Divinity which our form nature hides
b) to unveil the light
c) to reveal the Father (Spirit) through the Son (soul) and express Divinity through the medium of form (matter)

4. **The Christ.** Here the name is used as a *title* or *office*. For example, we speak of the *President* of the United States. When a new President is elected, he, too, is called the President. In like manner, the Christ is the name of the office of the Head of the Hierarchy. When the Head of the Hierarchy leaves this office and passes on to a greater office, the One Who will replace Him will be called *the Christ*. The Head of the Hierarchy, or the Christ, does not belong to any religion but

---

[1] Refer also to Romans 8:18-30.
[2] Please read Philippians 3:10-17 and Ephesians 2:4-11.

to the whole of humanity, to all religions, because all religions are inspired from the same source: the Hierarchy. No matter how they are distorted by human intervention, the light of the Hierarchy shines in them as a guidance toward beauty, goodness, and truth.

5. We have another Christ Who in old literature is called the symbol of perfection, **the Archetypal Man**, the perfect image of God. In the *Kabbalah* He is called "Adam Qadmon, the perfect model of all Form and of the first terrestrial Adam." As such He is the Cosmic Magnet attracting the terrestrial Adam and transforming him into His likeness. In the *New Testament* two Adams were mentioned: the first Adam, the Adam of dust; and the second Adam, the Christ, the New Adam, the New Man.

Eventually the first Adam, the average man, will develop gradually until the two Adams again become one, which means until the average man reaches the archetypal goal set for him for this cycle of evolution. In I. Myers' *Qabbalah* we read that "the Qabbalah names man as the purpose of creation and the first step is the upper Adam or Celestial Man."[1] (Zohar III, 48a)

We also have the term, "Christ Consciousness" which in esoteric literature refers to awareness on the Intuitional or Buddhic Plane.

---

[1] Myers, *Qabbalah*, p. 418.

11

▲ IN THE WILDERNESS ▲

WHEN JESUS entered Palestine, He was "twenty-nine" years of age. He did not go immediately to a city but retreated to the wilderness to prepare Himself for the great service which He would karmically render to the people. They were crystallized in the letter of their faith. He wanted to bring freedom to them, both physical and spiritual. The training through which He had passed previously had prepared Him for such a task, and He could easily regain His leadership and again become a great commander of the people of Israel. He spent long days and long nights in contemplation planning His work, and when He reached certain decisions and plans, He asked the Almighty One to lead Him.

Tradition says that one night, when He was contemplating His future labor, a Great One stood before Him, gave Him the salutation of peace, and said:

"No servant belongs to himself. Greater light and greater victory are achieved in greater renunciation. There is a greater vision than you have before your eyes.

Humanity is One, and your message will be the message of one humanity, one God. In the past you were crowned; at present, if you wish so, another kind of crown will be put on your head, and instead of jewels the drops of your blood will ornament it. The Temple that you built throughout ages must be destroyed, and you must be released from your riches to a greater freedom, to a greater revelation. I came here to invite you to decide if you want to renounce not only what you are, have, and know but also to renounce your plans, your beautiful body, the equipment of sensitivity, and your mental vehicle and dedicate them to One Who will use them for three years. Think and decide."

After a great crisis of decision, Jesus planned to dedicate Himself and all He had to the Plan of the Hierarchy and the service of humanity. He "decided to re-enact all five human initiations for the benefit of humanity." When His birthday came, He went to the river Jordan to be baptized by an initiate, a great disciple who was aware of the coming great drama and who was trying to prepare the public for the Great Labor.

In esoteric literature we are told that when a man, or a Monad, transcends the human kingdom and becomes a high degree Initiate, He can reach humanity in four ways:

1. He can *overshadow* or inspire His disciples.
2. He can appear in subtle bodies.
3. He can occupy the personality vehicles of a disciple and use them in the three worlds.
4. He can incarnate in a dense physical body if time permits.

In the first case a Master can overshadow His disciple or disciples, inspire them, strengthen them, and make them powerful agents in the fields of their service.

In the second case a Master may leave His dense body and appear in distant locations in His illusory body. Sometimes Masters can create more than one illusory body and appear in different locations simultaneously to deliver the same or different messages.

In the third case, when a Master has a disciple who has healthy bodies and a cultivated mind, with the disciple's permission He accepts the disciple's vehicle and renders a unique service where the disciple lives.

In the fourth case a Master can incarnate in those families from which He inherits good bodies and excellent opportunities to serve people.

Christ used all these techniques at various times to reach humanity. The three worlds referred to are the physical, emotional, and mental planes in which Masters may work if They so choose. The physical world here does not refer to the world of lowest matter only, but it also refers to the etheric matter by which many Great Ones manifest Themselves to come in contact with the physical world. In this case They appear as physical bodies but are not tangible.

Some Masters do not leave Their bodies at the Fifth Initiation, and They can walk among men in Their dense physical bodies. This does not prevent Them from appearing in Their etheric bodies when They want to contact Their disciples from a great distance. When this occurs, They leave Their bodies for a short time, as a man leaves his coat and later comes back to reclaim it.

In the third case the Great Ones choose a different method. They use the bodies of Their disciples for a short period of time to render some special service to humanity. In Tibet this is called *tolku*. The disciple offers his body to be used by his Master, vacates his physical body, and stands by in one of his subtle bodies. The Master occupies the body, tremendously glorifying it with His vehicles of the Spiritual Triad, and carries on His special service for the world in talking, acting, and anchoring a certain energy on the planet.

The real owner of the body stands by and watches all that the new operator does during His period of activity. The new occupant uses the body at certain times when He has to communicate with humanity or groups, or when He wants to perform a superhuman act. At other times the owner of the body can use it as he wants. There is very close cooperation between the owner and the occupant, and often there will be no apparent difference except at certain times when the new occupant will manifest greater beauties, greater power, and greater wisdom. The use of this method is very rare, and Great Ones train and test Their disciples before They attempt such a form of service. The most important requirement is purity of vehicles. This enables the disciples to hold the great charge of energy pouring in through the new occupant and use it for the divine Plan only.

Such an individual is very rare to find, except when the Master and disciple plan to work together and prepare Themselves for that task. In occult literature it is told that such an event took place between Jesus and His Great Master, Christ, in the river Jordan. Another disciple of Christ was there to baptize Jesus. John baptized Him in an ancient ceremony, and we are told that immediately after the baptism Jesus expressed His readiness to give His purified body for the great service. St. Luke says,

"And the Holy Spirit descended on him, like a dove, and a voice from heaven, saying, 'You are my beloved Son; with you I am pleased.'"[1]

What a beautiful way to veil a great mystery from the eyes of those who are not yet awakened to spiritual life! Christ was the *dove* and Jesus was His beloved Son, which means His beloved disciple closest to His heart. In esoteric literature Christ is called the Dove, the Prince of Peace. Jesus prepared His personality as the most beautiful temple to be used by a Son of God for the message and drama of the New Age. At that moment He became Jesus, the Christ. This does not mean that He lost His consciousness, but He stood aside in one of His subtle bodies and gave His mechanism to be used by Christ for three years. This was a great sacrifice and a proof that He was ready for a greater initiation. This event did not hinder His progress on the Path. On the contrary, because of His sacrifice and because of His extreme purity and beauty, He shared all the experiences of the One Who was working through His body, just as a man gives his car to another driver, sits by him, and shares in most of the experiences on the road and of the driver.

After the baptism we read that "Jesus was led by the Spirit to the wilderness." His Master Christ led Him to the wilderness to prepare the practical steps for the performance of the drama of Revelation. He remained there forty days, during which time He labored to adjust His bodies to the energy and power of Christ. Jesus didn't eat, didn't drink, and passed His days trying to appropriate His bodies to the energy and power of Christ. This

---

[1] Luke 3:22

was a time of testing of the instrument; a time of tuning in, fusing to such a perfect degree that Christ would be able to express Himself through Jesus, Who would remain a conscious witness of all that Christ did without creating the slightest obstacle to the service of Christ.

During these forty days the physical-etheric body and the mental body with the beautiful Chalice were re-tuned, tested again and again, until Christ was certain that They could act in perfect unison.

After this supreme preparation Christ left Jesus, and one of the representatives of the dark forces came to tempt Him. This was Jesus' last examination to test whether He was completely transformed or if there were still a human element that could mislead Him. The temptations were directed to His three bodies: the physical, emotional, and mental bodies.

At last no vanity, personal ambition, desire, pride, personal aim, nor separativeness was present in Him, and Jesus was able to overcome the subtle voice of temptation which followed Him and, as at the time of Zechariah, tried "to harm him."[1]

After Christ left Jesus, Caiaphas the High Priest visited Him. Through prophets and prophesies Caiaphas had known about Jesus, about His past glory and His future. For a few years he had tried very hard to make Him the uncrowned king of his people. "We are under the heavy yoke of Romans. We need to free ourselves from this slavery, and You are the one Who can lead us to liberation."

With a smile, after a few minutes of silence Jesus said to Caiaphas: "True liberation is the victory of the

---

[1] Zechariah 3:1

spirit over matter. Caiaphas, you stand for the Almighty One, for His creatures and you advise me to serve the transient interests of the people! I am here to serve the Lord and His children everywhere — not with political power but with the sword of Spirit."

"Jesus," said Caiaphas, "everything is laid at Your feet. We will all serve You. People adore You. You have the greatest popularity, and the people will follow Your instruction. We will be able to overthrow this yoke and proclaim You the King of our people!"

Jesus replied, "Get thee hence, Satan." And Jesus left him and disappeared behind the rocks of the wilderness.

It is very interesting to note that He used three Words of Power taken from the Holy Scriptures each time the evil approached Him. He said,

Man cannot live by bread alone.

You shall pay homage to the Lord your God and worship Him alone.

You are not to test the Lord your God.

There are profound mysteries in these words, and the student of Ageless Wisdom will be able to reveal them through meditation.

After this victory Jesus was ready to face the age-old battle against the accumulated crystallizations of the centuries: against ignorance; against worship of the golden calf; against hatred; against every kind of exploitation; against the misuse of energy, time, position, money; against all actions that create disunity or disharmony between the Almighty One and man, between Nature and man, between man and men, and between the real man and his vehicles of expression.

One day, early in the morning, Christ led Jesus into the field of His great ministry. "And Jesus, armed with the Spirit [Christ] returned to Galilee . . ." to teach beauty, goodness, truth, and simplicity.

12

▲ Initiations ▲

INITIATION is a process of entering into greater light, greater love, and greater power. It is a process of knowing and becoming.

The initiation ceremony is the "certificate" given to you as the approval of your achievements after you have labored, striven, sacrificed, learned, and experienced. Before taking any initiation, you should enact in your daily life all the requirements of that initiation. This means that before you are initiated you have to become an initiate. The most important achievement on the path of initiation is to know your goal, to approach that goal, to be proved by passing certain tests, and to enter the door by enunciating certain words of power.

Thus initiation is a steady process of enlightenment about your condition, your level, your abilities and possibilities, and a steady striving toward the goal. The goal may resemble a piece of music to which one must perform a specific dance, expressing the music through his emotional, mental, and spiritual life or activities. This is what a goal-fitting life means. Whatever you do on any level must carry you closer to your goal. The Great Ones lived goal-fitting lives and entered steadily into greater light, becoming the lights of the world.

We must mention also that the path of initiation is a path leading to greater fiery spheres where all earthly dross is burned and the unfolding human soul is purified as gold.

Helena Roerich, speaking about the fiery sphere, says,

> *One must remember that the transmutation of the organism and of the nerve centers must take place here, on Earth, amidst the spiritual struggles, amidst all the burdens and difficulties of life, amidst all the testing trifles of every day. Only this struggle evokes the necessary energies for transfiguration and the outliving of all the gross habits and attachment. The earthly life is indeed a purgatory, and without going through it, it is impossible to enter Paradise, or to come to the Brotherhood. The fires of the higher energies would burn the overloaded aura. The Community of the Brotherhood is too far removed from the ordinary earthly environment, and therefore it could not provide the necessary test conditions.*[1]

We are told that there are nine initiations through which the unfolding human soul reaches a Cosmic development and eventually comes in contact with the Fountainhead of Life which the Tibetan Master calls "The Central Spiritual Sun."

---

[1] Roerich, H., *Letters of Helena Roerich,* Vol. I, p. 202.

To better understand the life of Jesus and the main events through which He passed, expanding His communication with Existence Itself, we must discuss tentatively the seven initiations. <u>Initiations are stages of awakening, stages of greater response, of greater liberation and at-one-ment with the will of the Solar Life, and greater control over matter, space, time, and energy.</u>

The path of initiation begins when the son turns his face toward his Father's home. This is the beginning of the path of conscious evolution in which he steadily comes closer to his own essence, building better vehicles each time he takes a new initiation.

Initiations are divided into three sections:

    I.   from 1-5
    II. from 6-7
    III. from 8-9

The first five initiations are mentioned in many religions in allegorical ways. In Buddhism they are called

1. Farewell to the Home
2. Entering into the River
3. Enlightenment
4. Great Renunciation
5. Nirvana

In Christian literature they are known as

1. The Birth in Bethlehem
2. The Baptism
3. The Transfiguration
4. The Crucifixion
5. The Revelation

In esoteric literature

> the 6th Initiation is called Decision
> the 7th is called Resurrection
> the 8th is called Transition
> the 9th is called Refusal

In each initiation, the human soul unfolds through great experiences, meditation, service, and sacrifice. Each initiation may involve hundreds of years or even hundreds of lives, until the lesson is learned, responsibilities are faced, and the next door opened. The initiation process is like climbing mountains and descending into valleys, entering into light and darkness, refreshment and labor. For example, after the first initiation we have the massacre of the children and the escape; after the second initiation there is the temptation and the wilderness experience; after the Third Initiation came Gethsemane and Calvary, followed by the revelation of the entire drama. It is interesting to note that in each life man recapitulates his former achievements, as if in rehearsal, and strives toward the next great expansion. These successive rehearsals become easier and require less and less time. It is the new initiation that is the prime lesson to be learned and the greatest test to be passed.

The First Initiation. This is the increasing realization of the call of your Inner Presence. It is finding the pull of the true North or the attraction toward Goodness, Beauty, and Truth. Because of human imperfection, the initiate passes through dark nights and sunny days, trying to live the vision he has seen or the call he has heard in his heart. At the first initiation the greatest effort for the individual is the control of his physical body with its urges and drives. His next effort is service. He feels a powerful urge within himself to serve "and not exact due service," and he seeks "to love, not hate." This does not mean that he has become perfect, but he feels uneasy with his faults and unloving deeds and decides to battle the obstacles within him in order to retain his vision and the source of his inspiration. This is the birth of the light within the heart of the human being, and we are told that everywhere in the world thousands and thousands of men and women of every nation are taking the first initiation, thus forming the army of hope for humanity.

The first initiation is connected with the problem of economy, or bread, and we are told that the economic situation of the world will improve tremendously after humanity enters into the experience of the first initiation. Another important factor is that during the first initiation the initiate sincerely tries to sublimate his sexual energy and transmute it into creative and artistic urges.

The Second Initiation. This is called "The Passing of the River," or the ceremony of baptism in which man passes through a process of purification. Water symbolizes our emotional nature, and in this initiation the greatest labor is to control our negative emotions, glamors, and hang-ups. This is the most difficult task of a disciple. From life to life, through greater suffering and service he purifies his emotional nature and expresses only love, blessings, and compassion to all living beings. The virtue of harmlessness dominates his heart, and he strives to live a life of helpful service for all humanity. The heart center gradually unfolds and radiates its healing rays to those with whom the initiate comes in contact. This does not mean that he is in complete control of his emotional nature. The winds and waves still agitate his emotional nature, but he does not fall under their control nor does he take a negative attitude toward them. Using a spiritual technique he often keeps himself neutral. He insulates himself and watches these waves and winds and gains greater understanding of his nature. Once he becomes neutral to his own emotional agitation and negativity, the energy from his solar plexus passes to the heart center and man begins to think in terms of group. He becomes group-conscious, and he dedicates himself to group labor.

The Third Initiation or the Transfiguration. Buddhists call this initiation *Enlightenment* in which man gradually unfolds his mental powers, tries to penetrate into the laws of Nature, and has a vision of his true essence. It is during this initiation that the physical, emotional, and mental nature is flooded with a great light and energy coming from the Chalice and from the essence of man. This enables man to stand in the presence of his Angel, to have direct communication with Him, and to bring through service the Intelligence, the Love, and the Will energy to the world of men.

The Transfiguration Initiation is a great process of ultimate purification of all three bodies. As this purification continues, the threefold kundalini fire gradually climbs up along the spine and unfolds and vivifies each center, thus expanding the horizon of the Initiate into greater light, into greater vision, and into fuller responses to the Universe.

It is in this stage that man, the unfolding Spark, enters the process of becoming a conscious soul. He learns how to create thoughtforms of beauty to serve humanity and how to evoke energy from various centers within himself and within the Universe to further the evolution of all living forms.

When Buddha attained Enlightenment, He saw the Four Noble Truths, formulated the Eightfold Path, and dedicated all His light to the elimination of the cause of suffering and the leading of humanity into true freedom. We are told that He passed the Third Initiation with His Great elder Brother, the Christ.[1] It is very interesting to note that Moses, at this initiation, touched the Will of God and brought the Ten Commandments which were part of the Plan. It is in this initiation that the Initiate is "guided by the Hierarchical Plan" because he has built the communication line between his brain and the abstract mind where it is possible to touch the Plan. The Initiate is enlightened by intuitional and atmic energy through which straight knowledge is attainable. The light pours into the emotional and mental bodies, from the Intuitional Plane to the astral body and from the Atmic Plane to the mental body.[2]

In the *New Testament* the experience of the Third Initiation is given in a very beautiful analogy. It tells of a mountain — the initiation; there are the three disciples who symbolize the three vehicles of personality; and there is Jesus, the unfolding human soul. We have Moses and Elias. Moses symbolized the Will, the law, or the atmic vehicle; Elias symbolized the Intuition,

---

[1] The initiation which They took together occurred before the date upon which the Enlightenment of Buddha was recorded and Buddhism was established. Under the bodhi tree Buddha recapitulated His past experience of the Third Initiation.

[2] See *The Science of Meditation* by Torkom Saraydarian, p. 292.

prophecy, or the buddhic vehicle. At the Third Initiation the Chalice of Life with its nine petals is completed and man becomes a fountain of light, love, and power. He becomes a healer, teacher, and leader. The Tibetan Master says that the Third Initiation is the esoteric goal set before humanity. It is from this initiation on that man comes under monadic control, and his life has a definite direction toward the Highest.

The center which unfolds and controls the Initiate is the ajna center, which causes him to have psychic faculties. The Tibetan Master says that "it is not necessary nor advisable to develop the synthetic faculties, or clairaudience and clairvoyance, until after this initiation."[1]

When an Initiate has passed all tests of initiation and performed the labor required, he participates in certain ceremonials at which Great Ones officiate. We are told that at the first and second initiations it is the Christ Who officiates; He is the Hierophant. At the Third Initiation it is the Ancient of Days Who administers the Initiation of Transfiguration. It is after such a purification process that the Initiate may contact the Father, his Master, and Great Ones and may have a tremendous opportunity to unfold and serve humanity.

Christ once stated that no man can go to the Father except through Him. This means that no man can enter the Third Initiation and come in contact with the Ancient of Days, The Father, except by passing the first and second initiations in the ceremony and rituals of which the Christ is the Hierophant, the Initiator. He made that statement as the Head of the Hierarchy. The Head of the

---

[1] Bailey, Alice A., *Initiation, Human and Solar*, p. 87.

Hierarchy is an office and is called the *Christ*. Any qualified Master may hold the office called Christ, as the head of a nation holds the office of President or King.

The disciples and the followers of the inner circle referred to Christ as the Son of God. This was the title given to those Initiates who were permitted a closer relationship with the Ancient of Days. Those admitted to such a close relation are called Sons of God.

Christ emphasized that He is the Son of man so that people would not misunderstand the title given to Him as the Son of God. He wanted us to understand that He was a man who had achieved Sonship as we, too, may do if we proceed on the same path.

Orthodox Christians assigned to Him the title of "Only Begotten Son" and thus rejected all other Sons that the Father had such as the Buddha, Hermes, Zoroaster, Hercules, Vyasa, and others.

The true and pure service starts after the Third Initiation when a man enters into the path of Sonship, after the total purification of his threefold personality vehicles.

The Fourth Initiation. This is the Great Renunciation or the Crucifixion or the great Wilderness Experience. The Initiate is able to pass, by his own will, into the seventh or sixth sub-plane of the intuitional world and see things as they are and what they stand for. This is the path of great renunciation from personality aims and goals and of giving oneself to service for all humanity. Such a service enables the Initiate to stand in the light and presence of his true Self as an embodiment of love. At the Fourth Initiation it is the heart center that reaches its full blooming beauty and becomes a Chalice of harmony and beauty.

The most interesting thing that happens at the Fourth Initiation is the departure of the Guardian Angel[1] and the destruction of the Inner Temple or the Chalice. The One Who guided the steps of the Initiate since the individualization now departs, giving him a chance to delve deeper into the mystery of his own Self. Once the Causal Body or the Inner Temple is destroyed, man does not need to incarnate again in the world of matter. We are told that the Spiritual Triad, which is a center of intense light, love, and power, becomes the habitat of the unfolding human soul who now works through the highest head center, using the personality as the reflection of the Spiritual Triad.

Later on his path of evolution, when the human soul identifies with the Monad or when he achieves the monadic level, he will use the Spiritual Triad as a communication station between higher and lower worlds. The Fourth Initiation is the process in which the not-self gradually melts away and the Real Self emerges. The most powerful energy that pours from the Initiate is his all-embracing love, his compassion for all beings. It is this love that invites him "to give all and expect nothing."

The Fifth Initiation. This initiation is sometimes erroneously called the Resurrection Initiation, but according to esoteric tradition the Resurrection Initiation is the Seventh Initiation. The true name of this initiation is Revelation. The Tibetan Master says that

> *At the fifth initiation the great secret which concerns the fire or spirit aspect is revealed to the wondering and amazed Master, and He realises in a sense*

---

[1] See *Cosmos in Man* by Torkom Saraydarian, Ch. I.

incomprehensible to man the fact that all is fire and fire is all.[1]

In the Fifth Initiation the Initiate meets his Own Self as the embodiment of will and power, and we are told that He becomes a member of the greater Brotherhood of Sirius. He becomes a Master of Wisdom. The triple fire at the base of the spine is released and He stands as a shining culmination of agelong striving, sacrifice, and labor. The Fifth Initiation is the goal for humanity in our scheme,[2] but this does not mean that man cannot take further initiations if he works hard. Many Great Ones have passed the Fifth Initiation, and They are working on Their Sixth and Seventh Initiations, thus paving the way for the future development of our Race and of the living forms in our scheme. We call such Initiates *Masters of Wisdom* because They have experienced life in depth. They have loved and served, and now They know. They work primarily on the Intuitional Plane, and most of Their classes, called Ashrams, are formed on that level. Those human beings who sincerely love their fellowman and serve with love and patience often are invited to attend these classes, first on the higher mental plane and then on the Intuitional Plane, where the Wisdom of Ages is taught and the courage to serve the Plan is imparted to the disciples of the world. After attending such classes, a man has true "peak experiences" and his life cannot remain unchanged. We are told that in this initiation, the Initiate faces five great revelations:

---

[1] Bailey, Alice A., *Initiation, Human and Solar*, p. 174.
[2] See *Cosmos in Man* by Torkom Saraydarian, Ch. I.

1. The Plan of the Hierarchy is revealed to Him in its entire beauty and challenge.

2. The secrets of the Seven Ray energies and their triple aspects are revealed to Him, and He is given the power to use these energies to further the Plan.

3. "The mystery of the human soul" is revealed to Him.

4. The fourth revelation is the revelation of the Purpose of the Planetary Logos, and we are told that the fifth degree Initiate, a Master of Wisdom, for the first time can truly grasp the Purpose which is in the mind of the Planetary Logos. This is the Purpose referred to in the Great Invocation: "Let purpose guide the little wills of men, the purpose which the Masters know and serve."

5. The fifth revelation is the revelation of the mystery of the will-to-good, and Master Djwhal Khul says that "the significance of the Will-to-Good lies ahead of Him and will be later revealed."[1]

The Sixth Initiation. This initiation is called the Initiation of Decision, and the Initiate is known as a *Chohan*. We are told that after a Master has graduated into the Sixth Initiation He must choose between the Seven Paths of Higher Evolution to determine His field of service. We are told that every forty-nine years an opportunity comes to Chohans to make Their choice and

---

[1] Bailey, Alice A., *The Rays and the Initiations*, p. 645.

move to Their fields of service. One such opportunity came in 1903, another in 1952, and a third will come around the year 2001. Every time the Chohans make Their decisions, tremendous changes occur on the planet because of the energy They release or the energies They withdraw due to Their position on the planet, or Their relation to the planet or other centers in the solar system or the Cosmos. After the Sixth Initiation, the Chohan, if He chooses, may act in the "Center where the Will of God is known." The Tibetan Master says,

> *He can now express himself fully upon the monadic plane, the plane of universal life; the great heresy of separateness has slipped away from him and he knows nothing but love, unity, spiritual identification and a universal awareness. Because of this, he can become a creator, for creation is the expression of life, love and purpose, and all these three he can now understand and fully express.*
>
> *He is now an intelligent cooperator with the Building Forces of the planet and also of the solar system, and upon his chosen ray he will carry out his creative intentions.*[1]

Note: The Seven Paths of Higher Evolution are mentioned in esoteric literature as follows:

1. The Path of Earth Service
2. The Path of Magnetic Work
3. The Path of Training for Planetary Logoi
4. The Path to Sirius

---

[1] Bailey, Alice A., *The Rays and the Initiations*, p. 729.

5. The Ray Path
6. The Path on which the Logos Himself Is
7. The Path of Absolute Sonship

The Seventh Initiation. This initiation is the true Resurrection Initiation. In esoteric books we have some hints about it such as:

- The Son of God finds his way back to the Father and to his originating source at the Seventh Initiation.

- At the Seventh Initiation the consciousness of the universal life is His.

- At the Seventh Initiation, the Initiate wields power on all the seven energies or Rays.

At the seventh Initiation his vision penetrates beyond the solar ring-pass-not, and he sees that which he has long realised as a basic theoretical fact, that our solar Logos is involved in the plans and purposes of a still greater Existence, and that the solar system is but one of many centres of force through which a cosmic Entity vastly greater than our own solar Logos is expressing Himself. In these visions one great purpose underlies them all, — the revelation of essential unity and the unveiling of those inner relationships, which, when known, will tend ever more fully to swing the initiate into the line of self-abnegating service, and which will make of him one who works towards synthesis, towards harmony, and towards a basic unity,

During the Initiation ceremony, the opening of the eyes of the Initiate to see and realise, divides itself into three parts, which are nevertheless parts of one process:—

1. The past sweeps before him, and he sees himself playing many parts, all of which are realised to be but the gradual bringing of his forces and capacities to the point where he can be of service to and with his group. He sees and identifies himself — according to the particular initiation — with

    a. Himself in many earlier lives.
    b. His group in earlier groups of lives.
    c. His egoic ray as it pours down through many cycles of time.
    d. His Planetary Logos as He functions in the past through many evolutions and kingdoms in the entire scheme,

   and so on until he has identified himself with the past of the one life flowing through all planetary schemes and evolutions in the solar system. This produces in him the resolve to work off karma, and the knowledge (from the seeing of past causes) of how it must be accomplished.

2. The present. It is revealed to him what is the specific work to be done during the lesser cycle in which he is immediately involved. This means that he sees not only that which concerns him in any one life, but he knows what is to be the im-

> *mediate bit of the plan — involving maybe several of his tiny cycles called lives — which the Planetary Logos seeks to see consummated. He then may be said to know his work past all gainsaying, and can apply himself to his task with a clear knowledge as to the why, the how, and the when.*

3. The future. *Then, for his encouragement, there is granted to him a picture of a final consummation of a glory past all description, with a few outstanding points indicative of the major steps thereto. He sees for one brief second the glory as it shall be, and that path of radiant beauty which shineth ever more and more unto the perfect day. In the earlier stages he sees the glory of his perfected egoic group; later the radiance which pours forth from the ray which carries on its bosom the perfected sons of men of one particular colour and type; later again he gets a glimpse of the perfection of that great Being who is his own Planetary Logos, until finally the perfection of all beauty and the radiance which includes all other rays of light is revealed, — the sun shining in his strength, the solar Logos at the moment of consummated purpose.*[1]

---

[1] Bailey, Alice A., *Initiation, Human and Solar*, pp. 123-125.

13

▲ His Teaching in Palestine ▲

ONE OF THE CHRIST'S outstanding Teachings for the Aquarian Age was given in Palestine. With this Teaching He laid the foundation of the Kingdom of God on earth and opened the way for the fusion of humanity with Hierarchy. In the very near future, those who have directly heard this Teaching and those who in the past gave their lives for It may return to the world and demonstrate the Teaching in their own lives in all departments of human living, thus starting a great moral and spiritual revolution in the churches and in humanity as a whole. This may crack materialism, criminal exploitation of the masses, the great monopolies, and totalitarian dictatorship of all kinds. It may inflame the hearts of men and lead them toward compassion, harmlessness, simplicity, sacrificial service, and pave the way for the externalization of the Hierarchy, the Kingdom of God, on earth.

At present, man is the enemy of man. Men exploit men. Men still live by the blood of other men in spite of the colorful veil of so-called civilization and education. Because of this, humanity is on the edge of the abyss. It is very close to cutting its own life thread and ending its existence on this planet. Only by following the commands given in the Sermon on the Mount, only when the commands are lived by those who have in their hearts the fire of love for all humanity can humanity save itself from destruction. We believe that such people have started to incarnate in groups and already their influence is felt throughout our social systems. These incoming new age souls are vanguards of the Lord. When they reach a considerable degree of influence in human affairs and spread the spirit of peace, unity, simplicity, and beauty, the Lord will appear. It will be a tremendous day because in His Lotus Eyes, every human being will see his own essence, his future, and the path leading to Infinity.

> *In cosmic creativeness everything is built upon succession, since the roots of each structure are held by the law of Hierarchy. Each task and plan is built in goal-fitness, and they are affirmed by the great plan of evolution. Thus, all Our affirmations bring beneficent manifestations. Only attraction to the Chain of Hierarchy can reveal the path to Infinity.*[1]

A few verses from the Sermon on the Mount are quoted here for the convenience of the reader. No commentary is necessary because of their simplicity and di-

---

[1] Agni Yoga Society, *Hierarchy*, para. 164.

rect appeal to the Intuition. Each reader will interpret them on his own level and according to his own being-ness. They can be understood on all levels.

The blessed Mahatma Gandhi wrote, "The Sermon on the Mount went straight to my heart."[1] One day, when he was returning from a retreat, he read the Sermon on the Mount to thousands of people who were there to greet him and closing the book said, "Go and live as you heard."

> *Blessed are those who are pure in their hearts, for they shall see God.* Matthew 5:8
>
> *Blessed are the peacemakers, for they shall be called sons of God.* Matthew 5:9
>
> *Blessed are those who are persecuted for the sake of justice, for theirs is the kingdom of heaven.* Matthew 5:10
>
> *You have heard that it is said, An eye for an eye, and a tooth for a tooth. But I say to you, that you should not resist evil; but whoever strikes you on your right cheek, turn to him the other also.* Matthew 5:38-39
>
> *Whoever asks from you, give him; and whoever wishes to borrow from you, do not refuse him.* Matthew 5:42
>
> *You have heard that it is said, Be kind to your friend, and hate your enemy.* Matthew 5:43

---

[1] Gandhi, K. Mahatma, *An Autobiography*, p. 68.

But I say to you, Love your enemies, bless anyone who curses you, do good to anyone who hates you, and pray for those who carry you away by force and persecute you. Matthew 5:44

So that you may become sons of your Father who is in heaven, who causes his sun to shine upon the good and upon the bad, and who pours down his rain upon the just and upon the unjust. Matthew 5:45

When you give alms, let not your left hand know what your right hand is doing. Matthew 6:3

When you pray, enter into your inner chamber, and lock your door, and pray to your Father who is in secret. Matthew 6:6

Lay up for yourselves a treasure in heaven, where neither rust nor moth destroy, and where thieves do not break through and steal. Matthew 6:20

For where your treasure is, there also is your heart. Matthew 6:21

You cannot serve God and wealth. Matthew 6:24

You seek first the kingdom of God and his righteousness, and all these things [your needs] *shall be added to you.* Matthew 6:33

Why do you see the splinter which is in your brother's eye, and do not feel the beam which is in your own eye? Matthew 7:3

Ask, and it shall be given to you; seek, and you shall find; knock, and it shall be opened to you. Matthew 7:7

For whoever asks, receives; and he who seeks, finds; and to him who knocks, the door is opened. Matthew 7:8

Whatever you wish men to do for you, do likewise also for them; for this is the law and the prophets. Matthew 7:12

Enter in through the narrow door, for wide is the door, and broad is the road which carries to destruction, and many are those who travel on it. Matthew 7:13

O how narrow is the door, and how difficult is the road which carries to life, and few are those who are found on it. Matthew 7:14

Every good tree bears good fruits; but a bad tree bears bad fruits. Matthew 7:17

It is not everyone who merely says to me, My Lord, my Lord, will enter into the kingdom of heaven, but he who does the will of my Father in heaven. Matthew 7:21

This is my commandment: that you love one another, just as I have loved you. John 15:12

> *For whoever wishes to save his life shall lose it; and whoever loses his life for my sake shall find it.* Matthew 16:25
>
> *Whoever wishes to be great among you, let him be a minister to you.* Matthew 20:26
>
> *And whoever wishes to be first among you, let him be a servant to you.* Matthew 20:27
>
> *For wherever two or three are gathered in my name, I am there among them.* Matthew 18:20[1]

Only such a Teaching can save humanity from total destruction — when more and more people try to live according to it, making it the essence of their lives, and making possible the externalization of all those who are in tune with that Teaching. The whole purpose of His Teaching and activities was to establish the Kingdom of God on earth, but not by force, not by changing the personnel and political parties, but through inner regeneration and through spiritual birth.

It took Christ two thousand years to bring His Teaching to the attention of humanity. During that time many from humanity entered into the Kingdom of God, but still the Kingdom of God did not externalize on earth.

Churches sang and called Him "the King of Kings," but they failed to do His will. He did not want to be a king. He wanted each man to do the will of the King within his own being.

Did He fail? He did not.

---

[1] Lamsa translation.

Today, millions of people stand for peace, for one humanity, for one world. Millions of people strive for spiritual perfection, for closer communication with the Almighty One. Today, His star shines on the foreheads of millions of people. He set a vision that no power can destroy, and that vision eventually will transform humanity.

The externalization of the Hierarchy is inevitable. Already many thousands of disciples are entering into the seven departments of human endeavor, and soon these disciples will hold the highest positions. They are the only ones who cannot be bribed by money, position, or possessions or be overcome by fear or crime. They will create the field of understanding among all nations. These disciples will lead us to peace, simplicity, unity, and prosperity. They are those individuals who were trained by Him through the ages and sent out to prepare His way. In all nations and in all countries they speak one language — the language of striving toward infinity, toward peace, simplicity, love, and unity.

Within a few decades, the influence of these disciples will be so dominant that the average man will start to realize their vision and respond to it. This will bring an end to materialism and totalitarianism, and religious, economic, and political exploitation will be abolished. Because of this the dark forces are mobilizing all their strength to create disunity, war, distrust, lies, exploitation, and chaos in an intense effort to make Christ fail in His agelong mission. We are told, however, that the dark forces will be defeated, as they were defeated in the period from 1914-1945, *if* humanity moves quickly enough and takes the opportunity to fuse itself with the divine flow which started in 1975, working on a greater scale for right human relations and peace.

At the Wesak Full Moon of 1975, the Great Ones released the energy of the Will Center over humanity. The energy of Shamballa was released first in the Lemurian civilization, and from this energy came the birth of the fourth kingdom. The fiery angels dwelt in man then, and man was truly individualized.[1]

The second energy release occurred in the Atlantean civilization when the dark forces were battling the evolutionary forces. The release of Shamballa energy brought about the total destruction of that continent. The third release occurred from 1939 to 1945, during the period of World War II, the release of atomic energy, and the formation of the United Nations. The fourth release occurred in 1975, and the fifth will occur in the year 2000.

The Tibetan Master says that "the risks will then not be so great as in the first impact, owing to the spiritual growth of mankind. Each time this energy strikes into the human consciousness some fuller aspect of the divine plan appears."[2] This energy is fiery, highly dynamic, and penetrative. The effect will be conditioned by humanity which, through its activities, emotional reactions, and mental responses, will decide what effect this energy will have upon humanity.

Referring to some possible effects of the release in 2000, we can say that

---

[1] Read *The Science of Meditation* by Torkom Saraydarian, pp. 47-55, and *Cosmos in Man* by Torkom Saraydarian, pp. 169-172.
[2] Bailey, Alice A., *The Rays and the Initiations*, p. 716.

1. The sense of separativeness on the mental plane may be annihilated if enough men and women of goodwill strive toward unity and stand for the brotherhood of humanity. If this occurs we will see the sunrise of the New Age of unity and human brotherhood, with all the political, religious, and economic consequences, and Christ may reappear, revealing to us greater beauties.
2. If humanity continues in its hatred, exploitative attitudes, greed, and totalitarianism, a total destruction of our civilization through "fire" may be brought about. This does not mean that the human race will be annihilated, but the externalization of the Hierarchy will be delayed for thousands of years until humanity learns its lesson and turns to the vision of Christ.
3. If humanity does not respond to the virtues of the New Age — simplicity, beauty, love, and purity — but continues in its selfishness, this energy will hit the physical, emotional, and mental vehicles of humanity, creating many degenerative diseases.

We are entering into one of the major crises which may last a few days, a few years, or a few ages. Its effect may start immediately after 2000 like a thunderbolt, or it may be a gradual process.[1]

How must we face this crisis?

---

[1] Read *OLYMPUS — World Report . . . The Year 3000* by Torkom Saraydarian.

1. Daily meditate on the true meaning of the verses from the Sermon on the Mount given by Christ and try to adjust our lives accordingly.
2. Daily speak, write, and think about the brotherhood of humanity, about peace, non-possessiveness, and the highest good for humanity.
3. Three times daily say the Great Invocation and bless the United Nations and humanity.
4. Keep silence for one hour daily, and one day each month.

Thus we will meet the crisis and make it a door of initiation into the life "more abundant" for which Christ came.

14

▲ The Upper Room ▲

There are five great events connected with the Upper Room. The first is referred to in the words of the Christ:

Behold, when you enter into the city, you will meet a man carrying a water skin; and wherever he enters, follow him.[1]

The second is the mystery of the Holy Communion as described in the Gospels:

While they were eating, He took bread and blessed it and broke it, and gave it to His disciples, and said, "Take, eat; this is my body."

Then He took the cup and gave thanks, and gave it to them, saying, "Take, drink of it, all of you.

---

[1] Luke 22:10

> *"This is my blood of the new testament which is shed for many for the remission of sins."* [1]

The third is the ceremony of washing the feet of the disciples.

> *Then He poured water into a basin, and began to wash the feet of His disciples and to wipe them with the cloth which was tied around His loins....*
>
> *When He had washed their feet, He put on His robes and sat down; and He said to them, "Do you know what I have done to you?*
>
> *"You call me Teacher and Lord; and what you say is well, for I am.*
>
> *"If I then, your Lord and Teacher, have washed your feet, how much more should you wash one another's feet?"* [2]

The fourth is the Sacred Dance.

The fifth is the new commandment and deeper Teaching.

The first event refers to the Aquarian Age into which our sun is entering. The sign of Aquarius is represented by the water carrier who led the disciples to the Upper Room. The Tibetan Master says,

> *The sign for the Aquarian Age is that of a man, carrying on his shoulders a jar of water so full that it*

---

[1] Matthew 26:26-28
[2] John 13:5-14

pours over to all and sundry, and yet it diminishes not. The sign for this Law of Service is very similar, but the difference lies in this; that the man stands, perfectly balanced in the form of a cross, with arms stretched out and with the water pot upon his head.[1]

According to the Ageless Wisdom, Christ was the Water of Life carried within the pitcher, symbolizing Jesus, the son of man. The water symbolized the fire of the Intuitional Plane. Water is liquid fire. Buddhists call the Intuitional Plane the Buddhic Plane, the Plane of Enlightenment.

The Age of Aquarius is the age of enlightenment by the fiery water of the Christ consciousness. It is in this age that humanity will wash from its feet the dust and blood of the paths of the old ages through which it has passed in great suffering.

Thus with clean feet, with the intention of following the right paths of service and sharing, humanity will sit around the Table of Holy Communion and for the first time as a whole will be enlightened with the fact of the one brotherhood of one humanity. "The great spiritual achievement and evolutionary event of that age will be the communion and human relationship established among all peoples, enabling men everywhere to sit down together in the presence of the Christ and share the bread and wine [symbols of nourishment]," writes Djwhal Khul, the Tibetan Master.

As our sun is entering into the living waters or into the sphere of the fiery energies of Aquarius, the vision of one humanity, of one world, is emerging from the

---

[1] Bailey, Alice A., *Esoteric Psychology*, Vol, II, p. 120.

depths of our souls, and the love of the one brotherhood is becoming the motivating power of all our activities in all fields. In one of the great mantrams or invocations, we see this great aspiration of oneness. It says:

> *The sons of men are one and I am one with them.*
> *I seek to love, not hate;*
> *I seek to serve and not exact due service;*
> *I seek to heal, not hurt.*
>
> *Let pain bring due reward of light and love.*
> *Let the soul control the outer form,*
> *And life, and all events,*
> *And bring to light the love*
> *That underlies the happenings of the time.*
>
> *Let vision come and insight.*
> *Let the future stand revealed.*
> *Let inner union demonstrate and*
> *outer cleavages be gone.*
> *Let love prevail.*
> *Let all men love.*

As the influence of Aquarius increases and is recorded, digested, and expressed by the growing number of disciples, we will see the great flood of public opinion which will wash away everywhere in the world the desire to kill, fight, exploit, and enslave and which will usher in the true era of peace, joy, and spiritual blooming.

In the Upper Room Christ gave the vision of the New Age for which all His disciples should work. The keynote was humility, tolerance, service, and right motive. He esoterically gave their feet wings, like the wings on the heels of Mercury.

In the works of Philo we read, "All the powers of God are winged, being always eager and striving for the higher path which leads to the Father."[1]

Feet stand for labor and motive. When the motive is right, and there exists the labor — self-perpetuated labor — the disciple can be trusted with the great work of liberation. To indicate that washing the feet really refers to a cleansing of the inner motives of the disciples, Jesus said, "You are all clean, but not everyone of you." He was referring to the motive burning in the head of Judas.

Washing the feet of each other is a symbolic way of saying that you must watch with great humility the work each one is doing, *always* reminding each other of the *correct motive* behind all your labors.

We are told that people are initiated into a greater glory of understanding and labor because of their right motive — not because of their knowledge, power, or claims. Right motive means that you are in tune with the divine Will and have no obstacles or hindrances in your nature to prevent that Will from expressing itself through you. It is the motive that decides and controls the direction of your path, the direction your "feet" will take in the labyrinth of life. And, curiously enough, if the directive motive is right, everything else goes right. Remember also that the motive is the most *hidden* urge in man, and it is this hidden motive or urge that needs cleansing.

Only after such a purification of motives is the celebration of Holy Communion permissible. Holy Com-

---

[1] Yonge, *Philo's Works*, Vol. IV, p. 252.

munion actually is an act of realization that man can strive toward the source of all beauty, love, light, and power and be one with that source — not in wishful thinking, as are many churchgoers, but in conscious oneness which expresses itself in all-giving love and in fiery, intelligent service.

Every man and woman has a spiritual nature within, the radiation of which is called the conscience, the sense of responsibility, the urge to love and serve. This is the Master within, the Christ within. As we communicate and take communion with this Inner Dweller, it becomes the nourishing food, the nourishing energy, the life of our bodies. Eventually our whole nature transforms itself into the likeness of the Master within. This cannot be achieved unless the existence of such a Master is recognized within each of our fellow men and communicated through right relationships, respect, and gratitude.

Any expression, any act in any field and upon any level that creates disunity and separation is an act of sin. That is why Holy Communion, the conscious sense of unity and oneness in light, in beauty, in love, is an act of cleansing sin.

At the table He put the disciples in *contact* with each other and taught them how to communicate with Him in their dire need. This was so successful that even after a while they had no need for His personal presence. He was always with them, and they were in continuous touch with Him in their higher nature through inspiration, impression, or direct communication. The sacrament of the Holy Communion as celebrated in our churches is a faint memory of the supreme Teaching He gave to His disciples on how to contact Him without interruption. He taught the supreme science of contact, communication, or communion with each other and with Him. That is why each of His disciples was in communication with each other through some kind of spiritual wireless system. The continuous presence of the Lord was before their eyes. That is why they were so powerful and so in tune with each other and with the Lord — no matter where they were or what they were doing.

The washing of the feet was an ancient ceremony in which the Teacher purified the center beneath the sole of the foot. This center puts man in contact with the harmony of the planet. As he walks, he communicates with the pulsating life of the earth. He feels that he is walking on the body of the Great Life of the planet and gets in tune with Him, fusing and charging his body for greater service in healing and guidance.

The Holy Communion was a deeper mystery. The bread Jesus shared with His disciples was His heart center, full of divine love. He held his heart center in His hands and passed the flame of His love to each disciple, which expanded each of their hearts. Having asked them to join with Him in holding hands, He said,

> *This is my body* [the pure light of Buddhi, the True Love]; *receive it.*

After a while He again, in great solemnity, took the chalice, the cup of Jesus, and pouring into it the "wine" of the Spiritual Will passed it to His disciples saying,

> *This is my life, my blood. Drink it, so that you may be the forerunners of the New Age.*

The disciples drank the wine to express it as living waters pouring out of their hearts.

When this mystery was ended, Jesus gave them His last commandment of love and sacrifice. Then He ordered the table to be taken away and prepared His disciples for a Sacred Dance through which they were enabled to assimilate His Teachings not only intellectually but also emotionally and physically. Thus, the tuning-in with Him and the higher centers on the planet was made complete.

Then He said,

> *"Before I am handed over to them, let us hymn the Father, and so go out to what is waiting!"*
> *Having bidden us therefore to make, as it were, a ring holding each other's hands with Himself in the middle He said,*
> *"Reply with the OM."* [1] *So He began to sing a hymn saying,*
> *"Glory to Thee, Father," and we, going around in a circle said,*
> *OM*
> *"Glory to Thee, Word.*[2] *Glory to Thee, Grace."*
> *OM*
> *"Glory to Thee, Spirit,*[3] *the Holy One. Glory to Thy Glory."*
> *OM*

---

[1] Some translators use Amen instead of OM, which is the symbol of the Almighty One. Amen is the distorted form of OM or AUM.

[2] Refers to the Planetary Logos.

[3] The Solar Logos.

"We praise Thee, Father. We give Thee thanks, O light in whom no darkness dwells."
OM
"And for this reason we give thanks: I say, I will to be saved, and I will to save."
OM
"I will be freed, and I will to free."
OM
"I will be wounded, and I will to wound."
OM
"I will to be born, and I will to bear."
OM
"I will to devour, and I will to be eaten."[1]
OM
"I will to hear, and I will to be heard."
OM
"I will to understand, and I will to be understood as the Mind."
OM
"I will to be washed, and I will to wash."
OM
"Grace dances. I will to play on the pipe. Dance all of you."
OM
"I will to mourn. Lament all of you."
OM
"One Ogdoad sings with us."
OM
"The twelve above dance in time."

---

[1] This is the process of transmutation and transfiguration in which the lower self is devoured by the Christ within and manifested as service for others.

OM
"Whereon the whole begins to dance."
OM
"He who does not dance knows not what is going on."
OM
"I will to flee, and I will to stay."
OM
"I will to adorn, and I will to be adorned."
OM
"I will to be made one, and I will to make one."
OM
"I have no house and I have houses."
OM
"I have no place, and I have places."
OM
"I have no shrine, and I have shrines."
OM
"I am a lamp for you who look at me."
OM
"I am a mirror for you who think of me."
OM
"I am a door to you who knock at me."
OM
"I am a path for you, a wayfarer."
OM
"Now, respond to My dancing;
see yourselves in
Me as I speak,
and seeing what I do
keep silence on My mysteries.
He who dances understands what I am doing,
for you is this passion of Man,

which I am about to suffer.
For you could not wholly realize when I suffer,
had not I,
a Word,
come to you
from the Father.
Seeing what I suffer,
you have seen Me as suffering,
and seeing,
you did not stand firm
but were altogether moved.
Had you known how to suffer,
you would have been able
not to suffer.
Then know how to suffer,
and you will be able not to suffer.
What you know not,
I myself shall teach you.

"*You have me as a couch;*
rest upon Me.
Who am I?
You shall know when I go away.
What I now seem,
that I am not,
but what I am you shall see
as soon as you come.

"*I am your Lord,*
not the Lord of the betrayer.
I will to be harmonized
with Holy Souls.
Know you in Me the

▲ Christ, The Avatar of Sacrificial Love ▲

word of wisdom.
Say with Me again,

"Glory to Thee, Father.
Glory to Thee, Word. Glory to Thee,
Holy Spirit.
You have willed to know My
Word.
Once for all I rushed on
everything, and I was in no way
put to shame. I leapt forward,
but you, understand the all,
and having understood say,
Glory to Thee, Father."
OM
Then all sang Psalm 118 with tears and joy.[1]

After the sacred dance was over, He said to His disciples:

> *A new command I give to you, that you love one another, just as I have loved you, that you also love one another.*

Then He gave the most outstanding Teaching to His disciples, recorded especially in the book of John, chapters 14-17. The entire ceremony of the upper room was a great mystery in which only the twelve were invited to participate. The disciples' descriptions of that event were coded and deliberately watered down as a guide book for the disciples of the future.

---

[1] Refer to Mead, *The Hymn of Jesus*, and Greenlees, *The Gospel of the Mystic Christ*.

In concluding His teaching that evening He blessed His disciples, saying:

> *O Father, sanctify them in Your truth, because Your word is truth. Just as You sent me into the world, so I have sent them into the world. And for their sakes, I am sanctifying myself, so that they also may be sanctified in the truth. I am not making request for these alone, but also for the sake of those who believe in me through their word. So that they may all be one; just as You, my Father, art with me, and I am with You, that they also may be one with us; so that the world may believe You sent me. And the glory which You gave me, I gave them; so that they may be one just as we are one. I with them and You with me, that they may become perfected in one; so that the world may know that You sent me, and that You loved them just as You loved me.*
>
> *O Father, I wish that those whom You have given me, may also be with me where I am; so that they may see my glory which You have given me; for You have loved me before the foundation of the world.*
>
> *O my righteous Father, the world did not know You, but I have known You; and these have known that You have sent me.*
>
> *And I have made Your name known to them, and I am still making it known; so that the love with which You loved me may be among them, and I be with them.*[1]

---

[1] St. John 17:17-26

15

▲ GETHSEMANE ▲

AFTER THE LAST SUPPER was over, Jesus took His disciples to the garden of Gethsemane. He left eight of them in the garden, and with the remaining three He went into the woods. Then He said to the three, "Wait for me here, and watch with me," and He went further into the woods and entered into communication with Greater Ones.

The *New Testament* paints this event in Gethsemane with sorrow and pity. At first the witnessing disciples understood nothing because they were sleepy, and the impressions they had were translated through their feelings and through their fears of expected painful events and sufferings.

The Tibetan Master says that at this time Christ was between the Sixth and Seventh Initiations, "an interim of divine fusion."[1]

---

[1] Bailey, Alice A., *The Rays and the Initiations*, p. 722.

> *... Those Who dwell and work in Shamballa use this period to instruct the initiate who has made his decision through an expression of his divine nature and in the significance of the divine purpose; this concerns the relation of our planetary Logos to the solar system, and decision is made through the development of that highest sensitivity which leads inevitably to cosmic perception.*[1]

In passing, it is mentioned in the *New Testament* that on that occasion angels were ministering to the Christ. The key to the experience in the Garden of Gethsemane is found in the words He uttered:

> *"Father, not my will but Thine be done."*
> *The meaning of these words is not a statement of acceptance of pain and of an unpleasant future and of death. It was an exclamation evoked surely by His realisation of the universal implications of His mission and the intense focussing of His life in a universal sense. The Gethsemane experience was an experience uniquely possible only to those Sons of God who have reached this rare point in evolution.*
> *... It must be remembered that there is nothing static in the entire evolutionary process of our planet or of the cosmos; there is nought but process and progress, a moving on, an increasing attainment and a mounting achievement: To this great Law of the universe, even the Christ Himself is subject....*
> *He, too, moved on in His experience of divinity and*

---

[1] Bailey, Alice A., *The Rays and the Initiations*, p. 723.

is closer to the Father and to the one universal Life than ever before.¹

In Gethsemane He decided

> ... to take over the building or reconstruction work in Aquarius, and thus complete the task which He attempted to do in the Piscean age. He and His disciples and the New Group of World Servers are the pledged builders of the new civilisation, the new house of humanity.
>
> Something new, yet planned for from the very depth of time, happened then in that quiet garden; Christ, representing mankind, anchored or established the Father's Will on earth and made it possible for intelligent humanity to carry it out. Hitherto, that Will had been known in the Father's house; it had been recognised and adapted to world need by the spiritual Hierarchy, working under the Christ, and thus took shape as the divine plan. Today, because of what Christ did in His moment of crisis hundreds of years ago, humanity can add its efforts to the working out of that plan. The will-to-good of the Father's house can become the goodwill of the Kingdom of God, and be transformed into right human relations by intelligent humanity.²

Thus, as Jesus was passing into and through the Fourth Initiation, the great Renunciation, Christ was completing the Fifth Initiation and entering into the

---

¹ The Tibetan.
² *Ibid.*

Sixth. The Tibetan Master says that "at the time of the Crucifixion, the Christ took two initiations in one." This indicates perhaps that the Sixth Initiation, although undergone in a short space of time, is one of the most crucial points on the path of initiations, a testing point in which the Initiate has to *make a decision* based on all His past achievements and on visions of the future.

16

▲ Jesus and Apollonius ▲

THE HIERARCHY had scattered the seeds to be ready for the time of the harvest. The disciples knew their responsibilities and awaited the call to labor. All of them were sensing the Call. They were waiting for the voice to call them to labor. They were passing their time in Nature, meditating, contemplating, and following the "small voice" in their hearts.

On the inner side of life, Christ was in contact with all His disciples-to-be and with those who had a role to play. Most of them were not aware of this in their waking consciousness but were ready and willing in their subjective consciousness. In that state they were seeing the great task that was descending upon their shoulders. They knew Christ, but not in waking consciousness.

This is why when Jesus met His disciples on the physical level and told them to follow Him, they obeyed an inner drive, left their boats, nets, families, businesses, and followed Him without question. He gathered them one by one and initiated them into the mystery of the great drama of revelation and sacrifice.

The disciples were divided into groups of three, twelve, seventy, and five hundred. The mystery between Jesus and Christ was known to but a few of them. Some were Initiates; others only saw Jesus and felt the power radiating through Him. Three of the disciples, John, Peter, and James, were very close to Jesus. He instructed them in the mountains, in deserts, and at seashores to be the great dispensers of the Water of Life. He did not teach them philosophy or religion. He revealed to them what man is, what his goal is, and the techniques of how to attain that goal and serve humanity. These were the greater mysteries that He unveiled to His closest disciples. He opened their eyes to see their true Selves, and through their Selves the mystery of the Heart of God and the Will of God.

Jesus trained His immediate disciples to experience the fact of immortality. He galvanized them with the power of courage and fearlessness. He taught them about the transiency of material possessions and the value of freedom from attachments. He taught them how to come in contact with their own Souls and go beyond to the secret chamber within themselves where they could meet their Real Self. He opened their ears to hear His commands and opened their eyes to see His eyes as long as they stayed on the path of service. He taught them the science of sacrifice, the science of service and above all the science of unconditional love.

He trained them to be simple and beautiful in all their expressions and relationships. He taught them the secrets of silence and kept them silent until they learned to talk without hurting, without vanity and self-pride. He spoke to them about the life eternal and about the endless progress of the human soul toward the Cosmic Infinity.

He trained them and tested them until He was convinced that they were able to go and spread the Teaching of Light without mixing it with illusions and darkness. "And He gave them power and authority to overcome all the devils and cure disease, and sent them to proclaim the kingdom of God and heal."[1]

Jesus was a disciple of Christ. He was silently following the profound instructions of Christ. One day Christ told His three disciples to follow Him to a high mountain, and there took place the ceremony of the Third Initiation for Jesus. This was their most profound experience.

It it interesting to note that initiation is a process. It is not an act of entering into light and immediately becoming the light itself. Rather it is like entering a path toward a goal, and every day, every year, every lifetime, trying to achieve that goal. The path of initiation is a continuous path of striving, transmutation, and realization. Jesus was experiencing this. He had started on the road toward the goal of the Third Initiation, and, under the pressure of the Light of Christ, He was just culminating His achievement and entering into the final round of the Third Initiation, the Transfiguration, before starting on the path of the great Renunciation, or the *via dolorosa*.

Jesus recapitulated the first, second, and Third Initiations and was aiming at the Fifth Initiation. Christ recapitulated His first, second, Third, Fourth, and Fifth

---

[1] Luke 9:1-2

Initiations and was heading toward the Seventh Initiation.

The Third Initiation. We are told that at the Third Initiation of Jesus "in the presence of the three disciples He was transfigured; His clothes became dazzling white, like snow. . . . And there was a cloud overshadowing them, and a voice out of the cloud said, This is my beloved Son, hear Him."[1]

It is in this initiation that the mental sphere of the Initiate is flooded with the light of the Spiritual Triad. The Tibetan Master says that ". . . our Aryan race . . . will see *the descent* of the Kingdom of God to Earth as a result of *the ascent* of so many upon the ladder of evolution."[2] We are told that

The Third Initiation is the result of a triple activity:

1. *The lower mind transmutes the physical body.*
2. *The Soul transforms the emotional nature and enables it to accept the rays of pure reason or Intuition, and,*
3. *The Spiritual Triad transfigures the whole personality with its physical, emotional and mental nature. It is in this stage that the will-to-good or the will of God is gradually unveiled to the Initiate.*

This experience gave His three disciples a completely new vision, a new courage, and a new insight into their future unfoldment and service.

---

[1] See Mark 9:2-7
[2] Bailey, Alice A., *The Rays and the Initiations*, p. 592.

Immediately after this experience, Christ spoke to His disciples about the Law of Cause and Effect and about the Law of Reincarnation, references to which were eliminated from the manuscripts by some of the "fathers." It was after this initiation that the field of service really opened in front of Christ. He was a great Magnet attracting crowds to Himself, creating a striving in their hearts, and preparing some of them for the first and second initiations.

Initiations cause transmutation within the atoms and cells of our vehicles. We are told that each of our bodies is formed of millions and millions of tiny lives. These lives are not all on the same level but are roughly divided into seven layers or seven frequencies. As we take initiation, the frequency of the atoms changes and they advance on the path of their evolution. The substance with the highest frequency in our bodies is called atomic substance or the atomic plane. The percentage of this atomic substance increases as we pass from one initiation to a higher one, and, as it increases, the vehicles become more receptive or impressionable to higher forces and subtler energies. The time comes when our four etheric planes are replaced by Cosmic etheric substance, thus putting us in contact with the intuitional, atmic, monadic, and divine worlds.

The Fourth Initiation. After three years of strenuous labor, service, and sacrifice, the time came for Jesus to take His Fourth Initiation. The Fourth Initiation — derived from accumulated age-long detachments, renunciations, and sacrifices — is one of the most mysterious initiations. In the Fourth Initiation the Lotus in the higher mind reaches its maximum beauty, and the innermost petals begin to open with an intense fiery radiation. The Initiate becomes a burning bush of sacrifice and bliss. In the Ageless Wisdom this Lotus is called the Causal Body, the Temple of Solomon, or the Temple Made Without Hands. It is a center in the mental body for three kinds of energy: will, love, and light. The petals extend into each vehicle, carrying these three divine energies.

The Lotus is called a temple because in it is anchored the Solar Angel, the Inner Presence. It is also called the Causal Body because within that body are found the seeds[1] of the other vehicles. When man passes away, he leaves his physical, etheric, emotional, and mental bodies. On his return to earth in his next incarnation, it is these seeds which will bring the bodies into manifestation according to their own content. At the Fourth Initiation this Causal Body is destroyed and the Initiate is now free from the physical, emotional, and lower mental vehicles.

Many of the Masters keep Their physical bodies after the Fourth and Fifth Initiations as a car that can be used when needed. At other times They leave them in a safe place and use Their subtle bodies. They preserve Their physical bodies for certain services. Their bodies are built of higher atomic substance and are completely under their control. It is in this Initiation that the "death of all astral control over the human being" is consummated, and the Initiate no longer needs the body of glamor, the astral body.

At the Fourth Initiation Jesus learned to overcome death. People erroneously think that the Fourth Initiation

---

[1] See Chapter XII in *The Science of Becoming Oneself* by Torkom Saraydarian.

is the event of Crucifixion itself. This is not true. The great Renunciation, or the wilderness experience, is only the symbol of a process through which the Initiate passes. His most important lesson is to learn

1. To stand between matter and spirit and balance them in greater harmony.
2. To overcome the tendency to decay of all the little lives in his vehicles and to induce them to live should He temporarily vacate the body.
3. To release the Presence and graduate into Soul-consciousness and to work within the energies of the Spiritual Triad.
4. To function within the world through the higher mental plane and handle constructively the energies received from higher sources. He learns the mystery of the Fourth Ray energy, its effect upon the human kingdom, and how to handle it through the power of the Second Ray energy which is pure love.

The history of humanity and its future are conditioned by the energy which creates "first conflict, then renunciation and finally emancipation, as the Initiate perceives the Plan, takes participation in the Purpose and tries to prevent the evil."

The divine Purpose for this solar system is formulated in the Cosmic Mental Plane in the mind of that great Life known as the Solar Logos. This Purpose is formulated by relating the evolution of the Cosmos to the conditions within the solar system.

To a certain degree this Purpose is visualized by the Planetary Logos Sanat Kumara, Who furthers the evolution of the kingdoms of Nature accordingly. Sanat Kumara periodically contacts the Council in Shamballa and keeps it informed as to the divine Purpose. To use a metaphor, this Purpose is a vision of the evolutionary process to come, a rate of vibration, a note to which all creation must be tuned. Purpose is passive; and this passive Purpose is put into action and transformed into a Cosmic Magnet through the energy of the divine Will pouring out of the Head Center of the Solar Logos.

The origin of this divine Will is found on a still higher plane which is called the Cosmic Atmic Plane.

Our Solar Logos is on the way to achieving His Third Cosmic Initiation in order to be able to use this energy in its Cosmic sense.

On our planet we have two groups:

> The Custodians of the Will
> The Registrants of the Purpose

The Custodians of the Will draw the energy of the divine Will into Shamballa. The second group contacts the Purpose and registers it in Shamballa. Thus the Head Center of our planet is the treasury of the divine Purpose and Will, which forms a fiery magnet drawing to itself all lives on the path of evolution. The divine Will is latent in all Nature, but only a Third Degree Initiate can truly contact and use it consciously and purposefully. The Purpose is contacted then by the Masters and Their Ashrams, resulting in the formulation of a Plan whereby all kingdoms proceed according to the Purpose of Shamballa and the Will of the Central Spiritual Sun.

The Plan as a whole exists upon the Intuitional Plane. Those disciples or initiates who contact the Plan through meditation can, in their uplifted moments, create a mental response or drive which turns into a life intention, mobilizing all their thoughts, emotions, and activities and leading them toward the fulfillment of the Plan and the expression of the divine Purpose through the exercise of their willpower.

The agelong *intention* of Jesus took Him to the revelation of the Plan in its totality. He passed through great training and discipline to prevent evil and to renounce everything that was not in harmony with the Plan. Thus, Jesus culminated His Fourth Initiation upon the Cross with a supreme example of intention, sacrifice, and love for humanity as a whole.

The Will of Sanat Kumara is relatively unchangeable. The Purpose in Shamballa grows and unfolds as the centuries pass. The Plan of the Hierarchy changes periodically. These achievements and changes are due to the spiritual unfoldment of the Great Ones involved in Shamballa and in the Hierarchy. As the Masters proceed on the path of greater evolution, Their responses and awareness deepen and They improve and adjust Their formulation. Another factor in that change is the response of lower kingdoms. As they progress, greater adjustments are made, particularly in the Plan of the Hierarchy. The evolution of man depends on his steady penetration into the realm of the Plan and his knowledge of the Purpose in Shamballa. He becomes a spark of fire within the fiery Will of God.

The gospels contain much incorrect and misleading information about the events following Jesus' crucifixion. The occult records tell us that the Roman soldiers who were elected to take part in the drama unconsciously erected three crosses, each one representing four zodiacal signs. The twelve arms of the three crosses are for the twelve disciples. The middle cross was for Jesus. The soldiers tied Jesus' arms, feet, and legs, and they drove nails through His hands. . . . As darkness descended, people returned to Jerusalem. But a few of His disciples, including John and His Mother, remained to keep watch over Him as He was passing through an intense suffering.

As the blood decreased in Jesus' body, dropping out of the wounds in His head and hands, He slowly came out of His body and saw the miracle of the ages: a Chalice with twelve petals above His head and with a crown of thorns. He saw a white-blue central fire in it, which was bubbling and slowly penetrating from petal to petal toward the edges. When the blue and white glow of fire passed the boundaries of the petals in an amazing conflagration, the whole Chalice melted into the blue sphere in which He saw a Presence holding to His heart a triumphant warrior. The Presence touched Jesus' forehead and said farewell. . . . In a flash of time, Jesus identified Himself with the warrior and felt a great pain, a pain "in spirit," because of the departure of that Presence. When Jesus saw the destruction of the Inner Temple and the departure of the agelong Guide from Him He said, "Why are you forsaking me?" This was His last renouncement. But a second later He felt divine bliss filling His whole being because He met Himself, within Himself, as a triumphant warrior.

While He was going through such a rare experience within the sphere of His higher mind, His body was bleeding, the sun was setting, and a few of His beloved ones, including the Holy Mother, were watching Him. The curtain in the Temple was falling apart and unveiling the Inner Sanctuary, the Holy of Holies within man and within Nature. It was at this moment that in tremendous joy He announced His victory to the world.

"It is accomplished!"

The agelong labor aiming toward the release of His Inner Presence and entrance into the stage of His Beingness was finished and now greater paths were opening for Him. This is but a glimpse of the glorious initiation through which He passed to become a Fourth Degree Initiate.

During this time a more mysterious process was taking place on higher levels of divine existence. Christ was standing in front of the Ancient of Days and passing through the Sixth Initiation of Decision and preparing Himself for the Seventh Initiation. No human mind can penetrate the heights of such beauty, such an experience of freedom and responsibility. The Tibetan Master says of this event,

> *Great as is this mystery to you, and impossible as it is for you to comprehend that whereof I speak, it is wise to establish the fact in your consciousness that at the Crucifixion initiation, the Master Jesus took the fourth initiation and the Christ took the sixth initiation. The Master Jesus reached the culminating experience of the Lighted Way, whilst the Christ made that final effort which enabled Him entirely to complete and traverse the "rainbow bridge" and to "go to the Father" . . . thus moving forward on to the first stage of the Way of the Higher Evolution.*[1]

---

[1] Bailey, Alice A., *The Rays and the Initiations*, p. 524.

This first stage was the decision Christ had to make, choosing one of the Paths of Higher Evolution as listed in Chapter 12. He not only took the Sixth Initiation but also repeated the Fifth while Jesus was experiencing the Fourth Initiation. Here we see that it is Jesus Who was passing through the crucifixion experience and not Christ. The people crucified Jesus. This was the second great sacrifice that He made for the cause of humanity and the Hierarchy. The first sacrifice was lending His body to Christ.

In the *Koran* you will find the most complete records of this fact. For example, prophet Mohammed says, "They slew Him not, and crucified Him not, but He was represented to them by one in His likeness, and, verily, they who disputed about Him were in doubt concerning this matter."

The ceremony of the Fourth Initiation took seven hours while He was hanging on the cross. Most of the disciples thought He was dead. But when Joseph of Arimathea and Nicodemus examined the body, they were greatly moved as they saw that He was still alive. Joseph of Arimathea hurried to Pilate and asked for the body of Jesus before the soldiers could break His legs. It was customary that the legs should be broken before the body was taken down from the cross as proof that life was gone from the crucified one.

While John, the beloved disciple, was watching the cross, a messenger came from Pilate and asked the waiting centurion whether Christ was really dead. The centurion replied, "He is dead; that is why we did not break his legs." Then a soldier struck his spear into Jesus' side. Blood and water came out of the wound, but the body did not show any sign of sensation. The messenger returned to Pilate to report that Jesus was dead. A short time later Joseph and Nicodemus received permission to take the body of Jesus from the cross and bury it in the sepulchre belonging to Joseph which was hewn into the rock not far from the place of crucifixion.

After Joseph and Nicodemus arrived with the permission to take the body of Jesus, many women hurried to the place with healing herbs and very cautiously untied the bonds, took the nails out of His hands, and laid Him on the ground. They spread healing spices and salves on the wounds and all over His body to enable Him to return to His normal consciousness after such a terrible shock. Then they laid the body in the sepulchre. They smoked the grotto with aloe and other strengthening herbs and balsam and placed a large stone in front of the sepulchre to prevent possible intervention. Some Essenes who were great healers assisted Joseph and Nicodemus.

Early the next morning, the disciples found Jesus moving and uttering a few words. Seeing Him alive, the hearts of his beloved disciples burst, and they whispered in tears to each other and said, "He liveth!" This word was passed from disciple to disciple. With great joy and tears, it was spread to all the people.... "He liveth!"

Master Djwhal Khul says that

> *... Master Jesus arose out of the tomb; the chains of death could not hold Him. At that time of His "rising," a far more important event took place and the Christ passed through the seventh Initiation of Resurrection and returned back to His original state of Being — to remain there throughout all the eternities. This is the true and final resurrection. The*

Son of God has found His way back to the Father and to His originating Source, that state of Existence to which we have given the name Shamballa.[1]

Jesus lived with His disciples for eleven years, preparing them for their great mission. Christ often appeared to them and gave rare Teachings and initiated them into greater mysteries. When Jesus saw that His disciples were ready to carry His message to the world even at the expense of their lives, He left them in Jerusalem and went to India. There He preached for a few years and left His body in the mountains. Very soon He was born in Tyana to Cretan parents. He was called Apollonius of Tyana. Some people believe that He had a Greek body, but the esoteric record says that He had a Syrian body. He has kept the same body and is living in the Middle East in certain mountains.

The dates of the births of Jesus and Apollonius have been recorded as very close to each other, but esoteric sources say that there is a one hundred and five year error in the date of the birth of Jesus. According to these sources He was born in 105 B.C. "during the consulate of Publius Rutilius Rufus and Gracus Mallius Maximus."[2] His mission in Palestine ended when He was "thirty-three" years old. He left the tomb in 72 B.C. and lived a long life in various places in the Middle East and in India.

In the book *Heart of Asia*, professor Nicholas Roerich says,

---

[1] Bailey, Alice A., *The Rays and the Initiations*, p. 730.
[2] See *Esoteric Christianity* by Annie Besant, p. 129.

▲ JESUS AND APOLLONIUS ▲ 155

About six miles from Kashgar is the Miriam Mazar, the so-called tomb of the Holy Virgin, Mother of Christ. The legend relates that, after the persecution of Jesus in Jerusalem, Miriam [Mary] fled to Kashgar, where the place of her burial is marked by a mazar [tomb], worshipped up till today.[1]

... The Moslems of Srinagar told us that the crucified Christ — or, as they call Him, Issa [Jesus] — did not die on the cross, but only lost consciousness. The disciples took away His body, secreted it and cured Him. Later, Issa was taken to Srinagar, where He taught the people. And there He died. The tomb of the Teacher is in the basement of a private house. It is said that an inscription exists there stating that the son of Joseph was buried there. Near the tomb, miraculous cures are said to take place and fragrant aromas to fill the air.[2]

In His incarnation as Apollonius of Tyana, Jesus became a Master of Wisdom and took the Fifth Initiation. Those who read the life of Apollonius will find a tremendously beautiful similarity between his life and the life of Jesus Christ.

Apollonius led a victorious life as a Fifth Degree Initiate, and all His Teachings paralleled the Teachings of Christ. Jesus' followers in Greece and Italy fanatically fought and burned much of the wisdom Apollonius had left to the world, believing that His Teaching was differ-

---

[1] Roerich, Nicholas, *Heart of Asia*, p. 39.
[2] *Ibid.*, pp. 22-23.

ent from what Christ had taught in Palestine. But Apollonius' followers in Greece and Rome were more tolerant and wiser and never disputed what Jesus had taught in Palestine.

Some of the disciples knew of this mystery. In Greece they spread the story of His life in Palestine. Eventually two separate stories were told — one in Greece and the other in the Middle East — with the same content but referring to different personalities. The gospel narratives and letters describe both as one under the name of Jesus. It would make no difference if the words and acts were presented under the name of Apollonius. Actually what He did in Palestine was continued in Greece and Rome with greater power. Some people tried to find contradictions and differences in the narratives but there are none, as Appollonius was the continuation of Jesus, and the events happened in different ways on separate occasions.

In Greece He used a slightly different method of teaching. He emphasized simplicity, beauty, and truth without any reference to Judaic or dogmatic religion and without making any reference to any existing faith. He created no conflict between what He had previously taught and what He presented at that time. He saw only the beauty, the simplicity, and the truth and drew the attention of the people to these three great fundamentals without coloring them.

For three years in Palestine Jesus was preparing Himself to become a pure channel for the Christ's Teaching, the Teaching of Salvation, but His own individuality interfered on occasion and Christ's Teaching had elements of Jesus, too. This made Their Teaching human and divine, traditional and new, but toward the end of Jesus' life in Palestine He yielded Himself more and more to Christ, becoming an uninterrupted channel for His Teaching. After a long life of healing, teaching, service, and sacrifice, He was led by Christ to the Himalayas to enter into the gate of His Fifth Initiation, which is called the Revelation, while Christ entered into His Seventh Initiation, the true Resurrection.

Jesus became a Master of Wisdom, came back, and preached the wisdom of Christ. He kept the fire of the true spirit of Christ in all Christian churches. After the Fifth Initiation He was completely in "Christ Consciousness," and His Teaching was tremendously expanded, simplified, and deepened by the fact that the great overshadowing One was now a Seventh Degree Initiate Who was able to penetrate "beyond the solar ring-pass-not" and was able now to work "towards synthesis, towards harmony, and towards a basic unity."[1]

We are told that a Fifth Degree Initiate is one who "ascends with the Heavenly Man [the Planetary Logos]" to the Atmic Plane, and at the Seventh Initiation "he dominates the entire sphere of matter contained in the lowest cosmic plane [the Cosmic Physical], escapes from all etheric contact, and functions on the cosmic astral plane."[2]

Apollonius had reached this stage. The overshadowing One was a Seventh Degree Initiate, and Apollonius Himself surpassed the human kingdom and, through the Fifth Initiation, entered into the Kingdom of God. He had demonstrated His love toward man and God, and

---

[1] See Bailey, Alice A., *Initiation, Human and Solar*, pp. 123-124.
[2] Bailey, Alice A., *A Treatise on Cosmic Fire*, p. 121.

now He was a Master, over-shadowed by the Prince of Peace, the Christ.

He was "very beautiful to look upon" and also very gentle. In Greece He entered into many mystery Temples and added His wisdom to their Teaching. For Him religion was a service, an experience, and an achievement — not a faith only. He had conquered time and space and He was able to see the future, be in the future, and yet command the present with the authority of the future.

Legends say that He was born in Tyana, "a town in southern Cappadocia, in the mid-eastern part of Asia Minor," by a Cretan mother. It is very interesting that His biographer says that He was born at the winter solstice of a virgin, that angels appeared, and so on. He was very intelligent and extremely handsome. He studied philosophy and became a close friend of the priests of the various temples in Greece and Rome and was initiated into their mysteries. The priests loved Him because He was able to see in their Teaching the common denominator. He ate only fruits and vegetables, did not drink wine, went barefoot, let His hair grow long, and dressed in linen. Once He took a vow of silence for five years. He traveled to Rome, Crete, Greece, Babylon, Nimus, Antioch, Selencia, Asia Minor, Spain, Africa, Egypt, Nepal, and the Ganges, visiting temples and monasteries of wise men. All this time He was overshadowed by the Christ and impressed by Him to further His evolution and to serve humanity. "His teaching was pure. He healed the sick, cured the blind, even raised the dead men to life, cast out demons, stilled tempests and prophesied the future events...." He had disciples but He left them freedom in their choice of life and never imposed His mode of life on others. "Apollonius was worshiped in the beginning of the fourth century under the name of Hercules."

One of the church fathers, Justin Martyr, says,

> *How is it that the talismans of Apollonius have power in certain members of creation, for they prevent, as we see, the fury of the waves, and the violence of the winds, and the attacks of wild beasts; and whilst our Lord's miracles are preserved in tradition alone, those of Apollonius are most numerous and actually manifested in present facts, so as to lead astray all beholders?*

At sixteen Apollonius entered the school of Pythagoras and became his faithful disciple. Occultism says that Pythagoras is the Master K.H., Who is to replace the Christ 2500 years hence and become the head of the Hierarchy.

Once Apollonius wrote a letter to a father who had lost his son:

> *There is no death of anyone but only in appearance, even as there is no birth of any save only in seeming. The change from being to becoming seems to be birth and the change from becoming to being seems to be death, but in reality no one is ever born nor does one ever die. It is simply a being visible and then invisible; the former through the density of matter, and the latter because of the subtlety of being — being which is ever the same, its only change being motion and rest.*[1]

---

[1] Mead, G.R.S., *Apollonius of Tyana*, p. 149.

17

▲ Judas, The Iscariot ▲

THERE ARE MANY STORIES about this disciple all based upon traditions and emotional reactions to the events of the Crucifixion. Some say that Judas acted his part in the drama consciously as it was set for him. He betrayed Christ and sold his Master for thirty pieces of silver, hung himself on a tree, and at the time of the earthquake he fell down and was buried beneath the earth. If this were true, he was a great hero whose sacrifice was equal to or even greater than the sacrifice of Christ, as he was undertaking a role portraying himself as the worst of human beings throughout the history of humanity. Consequently, he was facing all the curses of the ages with conscious suffering for his Lord and for the Cause. According to other accounts, he betrayed the Lord because of his greed or betrayed Him when he felt that Jesus was not the Messiah whom the Jews had expected to liberate them from the yoke of the Romans. It is also said that he betrayed Jesus to discover if He really were able to overcome death and His enemies as He proclaimed.

According to another tradition, Judas was a dedicated servant of the Dark Lodge. He followed Christ step by step. Christ knew this and, out of His love and compassion and in His wisdom, He had an interview with him and accepted him as a disciple. Judas was very happy because this enabled him to keep a closer watch over Jesus and enabled him to hurt Jesus and His work.

Christ was happy, too, because He thought that in having Judas among the disciples, they would have firsthand knowledge about the subtleties of evil and thus would be trained to overcome them in their own nature and in the world. It would also be a tremendous discipline to continue their ascension toward light in the company of a servant of darkness who would keep them awake and watchful. Judas was elected to keep the disciples watchful toward their spiritual essences and to test them at every turn to discover if they could stand in light, love, and goodwill.

Even deeper than this, Christ's intention was to bring out to the utmost His power of love, the power of His wisdom over a dark brother, and make him a son of Light, thus achieving a greater victory than the victory over death. For three years His grace, His wisdom, His love did not penetrate the skin of Judas. As Christ was growing in greater light and influence, Judas was becoming more eager to hand Him over to death. And, as the records say, he betrayed Jesus.

It was in the Garden of Gethsemane that the miracle occurred. Judas came at midnight with soldiers of the High Priests, and as a sign to let them know who Jesus was he went ahead and said to Him, "Peace, Master," and kissed Him. Jesus said to him, "Is it for this that you have come, my friend? Do you betray the Son of Man with a kiss?"

At the darkest moment of Judas's life, Christ touched his heart. The fire of Christ penetrated into his body, his nerves, his being, and suddenly in nervous shivering he saw himself as he was. Then he saw the vision of infinite goodness and beauty and was hit by the lightning of love and was won by the forces of goodness. He left Jesus with the multitude who took Him to the house of the High Priest; he followed Christ step-by-step, coming closer and closer to Him. He shared all His sufferings, and through his sufferings the evil in him was gradually melted and crushed. Early in the morning, without sleep, he went to the house of the High Priest, bringing back the thirty pieces of silver, and said to them, "I have sinned because I have betrayed innocent blood." Then he threw the silver into the temple, and in his desperation he rushed into the sanctuary, destroyed many precious vessels, rent the curtain from top to bottom, and ran to Mount Golgotha.

In the dark records of his many lives, this was the first time that Judas saw the light and made a tremendous breakthrough toward reality. He came closer to the Prince of Peace, to the Head of the Hierarchy. Christ destroyed the evil in him and wiped away a station of evil which was acting through him for many lives and in many countries whenever the Hierarchy sent a messenger of light.

It was at the foot of the cross that Judas received his initiation. Tradition says that he was present when Jesus was beaten almost to death and when the nails were hammered through His hands. He was totally identified with Christ through his act of betrayal and, when most people departed from the area of crucifixion, he went near the foot of the cross and cried, "Lord!"

"Judas?"

"Lord, will you forgive me?"

"All is forgiven, Judas. Peace be with you. Peace, peace, peace. My love for you is greater."

Judas disappeared in the darkness, crying bitterly, but witnessing a great sunrise in his soul for coming eternities.

After the resurrection Christ appeared to His twelve disciples in the upper room where they were gathered, including Judas Iscariot. The twelve symbolized the zodiac. Christ was the heart of the Sun, and Judas Iscariot represented the sign at the time in power.[1]

In the past, Christ had given the philosophy of the Light of the path through *The Bhagavad Gita*. In Palestine, He translated the path as true Love. In the future, He will translate the true path as Will, as power.

---

[1] See Bailey, Alice A., *The Rays and the Initiations*, pp. 355-356.

18

▲ MASTER JESUS — PRESENT AND FUTURE ▲

There is also a group of devas connected with the Lodge of Masters, whose work it is to build the aspirational forms towards which average man may aspire. They are divided into certain groups — three in number — connected with science, religion and philosophy, and through these groups of deva substance the Heads of the three departments reach men. It is one of Their channels for work. The Master Jesus is particularly active at this time along this line, working in collaboration with certain adepts on the scientific line, who — through the desired union of science and religion — seek to shatter the materialism of the west on the one hand and on the other the sen-

timental devotion of the many devotees of all faiths.[1]

The Master Jesus will ... with certain of His chelas effect a re-spiritualisation of the Catholic churches, breaking down the barrier separating the Episcopal and Greek churches from the Roman. This may be looked for, should plans progress as hoped, about the year 1980.[2]

At this particular time [1922] the Master M., the Master K. H. and the Master Jesus are interesting Themselves closely with the work of unifying, as far as may be, eastern and western thought, so that the great religions of the East, with the later development of the Christian faith in all its many branches, may mutually benefit each other. Thus eventually it is hoped one great universal Church may come into being.

The Master Jesus, Who is the focal point of the energy that flows through various Christian Churches, is at present living in a Syrian body, and dwells in a certain part of the Holy Land. He travels much and passes considerable time in various parts of Europe. He works specially with masses more than with individuals, though He has gathered around Him quite a numerous body of pupils.... He is distinctively the Great Leader, the General, and the wise Executive, and in Church

---

[1] Bailey, Alice A., *A Treatise on Cosmic Fire*, pp. 677-678.
[2] *Ibid.*, p. 759. (Written in 1922. We now see great changes in this direction.)

matters He co-operates closely with the Christ, thus saving Him much and acting as His intermediary wherever possible. No one so wisely knows as He the problems of the West, no one is so closely in touch with the people who stand for all that is best in Christian teachings, and no one is so well aware of the need of the present moment. Certain great prelates of the Anglican and Catholic Churches are wise agents of His.[1]

The Master Jesus, the inspirer and director of the Christian Churches everywhere, though an adept on the sixth ray under the department of the Mahachohan [the Lord of Civilisation], *works at present under the Christ for the welfare of Christianity.*[2]

. . . the Christian, the Hindu and the Buddhist . . . will be intimately related, whilst the Mahommedan faith will be found to be linked to the Christian faith because it embodies the work of the Master Jesus as He overshadowed one of His senior disciples, a very advanced initiate, Mahomet.[3]

The Messiah for Whom [the Jews] *wait will be one of Christ's senior disciples, but it will* not *be, as originally intended, the Christ. . . . The probability is that the Master Jesus will assume (under instruction from the Christ) the part of the Messiah.*[4]

---

[1] Bailey, Alice A., *Initiation, Human and Solar*, pp. 55-57.
[2] *Ibid.*, pp. 46-47.
[3] Bailey, Alice A., *The Rays and the Initiations*, p. 254.
[4] *Ibid.*, pp. 705-706.

> *Upon the spiritual side . . . the whole field of religion will be re-inspired and re-oriented from Rome because the Master Jesus will again take hold of the Christian Church in an effort to re-spiritualise it and to re-organise it. From the chair of the Pope of Rome, the Master Jesus will attempt to swing that great branch of the religious beliefs of the world again into a position of spiritual power and away from its present authoritative and temporary political potency.*[1]

H. P. Blavatsky speaking about Jesus once said,

> *Once I was in a great cave-temple in the Himalaya mountains, with my master* [Master Morya]. *There were many statues of adepts there. Pointing to one of them, He said; "This is He whom you call Jesus. We count him to be one of the greatest among us."*[2]

---

[1] Bailey, Alice A., *The Destiny of the Nations*, p. 59.
[2] Blavatsky, H. P., *Collected Writings*, Vol. VIII, p. 402.

19

▲ Rending the Veils ▲

ACCORDING TO ESOTERIC LITERATURE there are three higher states of consciousness, three higher states of beingness in which the awareness of the human unit unfolds, develops, and reaches its divine maturity, enabling man to step out of the Cosmic Physical Plane. These higher states of beingness or awareness are known as the three Halls:

1. The Hall of Concentration
2. The Hall of Choice
3. The Hall of Blinded Men

Separating these Halls are four veils. The great Teacher, Djwhal Khul, speaks of these veils:

> *They are in the nature of opposing forces and energies which act as inhibitory factors to the aspirant as he seeks to make progress, and to the entire human family as it moves onward upon the Path of Evolution . . . ; they are essentially physical*

forces, and although they are the result of man's own effort and activity down the ages, they are largely unrealised, unseen obstacles to his progress. They constitute the lowest concentration of forces precipitated from levels of activity other and higher than the physical. . . . They lie between the subtle inner man, mental and astral, and his physical brain. They are that which prevents brain registration of the world of causes and of meaning. This inner world can be emotional or mental in its focus and in its force precipitation on to the etheric plane. It can be the fused result of personality integration and be a combination of energies; or it can be dominated by the effects of soul energy. These, if evoked, can penetrate occultly and drive out or break down and through the separating veiling forces, thus producing coordination eventually between soul and brain.

These veils are as curtains over the windows of vision. They prevent realisation of that which lies beyond the room or area of average or mediocre experience, and they prevent the light from penetrating.[1]

1. We have first the *veil of impulsion* which obscures the door leading to the **Hall of Concentration**. This is the veil which average man meets. This veil is the accumulation of maya, glamors, and illusions and often is called the Dweller of the Threshold. At the first two initiations man struggles with this obstacle. He slowly understands it better and, in the meantime, senses the Inner Guide within himself. The mystical marriage with

---

[1] Bailey, Alice A., *The Rays and the Initiations*, p. 195.

the Guide cannot take place until he rends this veil and passes through. This is his entrance into the consciousness of a Third Degree Initiate, consummated at the Transfiguration. We are told that Moses rent the first veil when He climbed the mountain where he met the Angel of the Presence and received the Laws.

2. The **Hall of Choice** is entered when the second veil is lifted or rent. This veil is called the *veil of distortion* and is related to glamors. After the glamors are entirely lifted up and cleaned, the Initiate enters into the Hall of Choice which leads him up to the Fourth Initiation, the Great Renunciation.

The Hall of Choice is related to the Fourth Initiation in which the Initiate will learn to stand on his own freedom between "the earth and heaven," renounce all that he has and all that he has been, and withdraw from the form life. This veil is called the *veil of distortion* because it presents a distorted picture of the reality beyond to the Initiate waiting in front of the veil. It is the body of glamors.

We are told that it was the Christ Who first rent this veil, ". . . from top to bottom" and let loose a great light on the second level of the etheric plane. This light has the nature of love; it was a new path between humanity and the Hierarchy. It would seem that, after he rends this veil, the Initiate enters into the second hall which is the Plane of Intuition, the Plane of Buddhi, or the Plane of Enlightenment.

The second veil, referred to in the *New Testament* as the *veil of the temple*, is rent at the time of the Fourth Initiation. It is the symbol for a precious vesture which hides the Monad, the Father, and is called the Lotus, the Chalice, or the Temple of Solomon. When direct communication between the personality and the Monad is achieved, the fire of the Monad rends and burns the veil, the Dweller in the Temple is released, and the unfolding human soul meets himself on the Buddhic Plane.

3. The **Hall of Blinded Men** is entered at the Sixth or Seventh Initiation, after the third veil, the *veil of separation* between the Hall of Choice and the Hall of Blinded Man is torn away. We are told that the rending of this veil creates a tremendous light by which the Initiate is blinded.

The Tibetan Master says that it was Saul of Tarsus who, when he saw the "Glory of the Lord," changed and became Paul, the Apostle. At this time he was able to approach the third veil and cause a minor rent which let loose a third kind of energy, the characteristic of which is synthesis. It is this energy which is causing union and through it a new civilization will eventually be built. With the rending of these three veils, we have three kinds of energy, "Law, Love, Union or Synthesis."

4. Another veil, called the *veil of aspiration*, will be rent ". . . as a result of the energies released and the gained good which the three earlier rents have made possible. This fourth major rent will be made by humanity itself, standing with 'massed intent,' focussed through the groups which are externalisations of the Ashrams of the Masters. It will therefore be made at the time that the Hierarchy takes physical shape upon the earth again."[1] The nature of the energy which will pour through this fourth rent may be called *Life*.

Each time that a disciple takes a new initiation, he makes the rent bigger and lets more light, love, and

---

[1] Bailey, Alice A., *The Rays and the Initiations*, p. 194.

synthesis into the race of men, enabling it to achieve greater spiritual realization.

These veils also have a protective effect upon human beings and upon the whole of humanity. They shelter man from burning energies which pour down from higher planes and may have destructive effects upon the human mechanism and upon our social environment if they are contacted and released prematurely.

There are planetary veils as well as the veils of individuals. When the Great Ones rend the planetary veils, They let loose upon humanity greater light, greater love, and greater synthesis, with their positive and negative effects.

At the present time, those esoteric groups which are working under the impression of the Christ are enlarging the rents in the veils and evoking creative and dynamic energies to the areas where they want the group impact to be felt. With their dedication, intention, one-pointed striving, unanimous and simultaneous meditation and service, they penetrate deeper into the veils of the planet. Such groups are providing greater light, purer love, and deeper synthesis for humanity.

Actually we have seven Halls mentioned in occult literature. Three of them are concerned with the personality; one of them is concerned with the Soul; the three higher Halls are related to the Buddhic, Atmic, and Monadic Planes.

1.	The Hall of Ignorance	physical plane
2.	The Hall of Learning	astral plane
		lower mental plane
3.	The Hall of Wisdom	higher mental plane
4.	The Hall of Concentration	sphere where the Soul is

5. The Hall of Choice   Buddhic Plane
6. The Hall of Direction   Atmic Plane
7. The Hall of Monadic Light   Monadic Plane
                               and beyond

Between these planes we have eight etheric planes. The first four are the four lower ethers. The second four are the Cosmic Ethers — Buddhic, Atmic, Monadic, and Divine Planes. It is after this last plane that the Cosmic Astral Plane opens in front of the eyes of the great Initiate.

Within these ethers we have various veils and webs. For example, within the fourth etheric plane we have etheric webs:

> *These circular disks or webs are to be found between each pair of the centres up the spine and also in the head. They are normally dissipated as purity of life, the discipline of the emotions and the development of the spiritual will are carried forward.... The webs in the head are of much higher quality and bisect the skull horizontally and vertically.*[1]

We also have webs between the physical and astral planes, between the astral and mental, and so on. For example, when the web separating the etheric and astral planes is burned away by the increasing fire of the spiritual man, the three lower bodies — physical, emotional, and mental — function as one unit. Greater

---

[1] Bailey, Alice A., *Esoteric Healing*, pp. 186-187.

unity is achieved when the web between the mental and Intuitional Planes is burned away at the Fourth Initiation.

Let us remember that

> *The etheric web which is found between the centres in the spine, and which is found at the top of the head (protecting the head centre), is destroyed in man's mechanism by the activity of certain forces found in that mysterious fire which we call the kundalini fire. The cosmic rays ... constitute aspects of the planetary kundalini, and their effect will be the same in the body of the planetary Logos, the Earth, as it is in the human body; the etheric web between the physical and astral planes is in process of destruction, and it is of this event which the sensitives of the world and the spiritualists prophesy as an imminent happening.*[1]

The web between the second and third sub-planes of matter prevents continuity of consciousness between the physical brain and the astral world. We are told that when a man reaches that point of development where he begins to see the fourth lower ether, the disintegration of this web starts, and the man achieves continuity of consciousness between the physical brain and the astral world. He now has the right to work there to eliminate the source of glamor and evil.

Similarly, we have other webs on the second and third sub-planes of the mental, Intuitional, and Atmic Planes. By eliminating these veils, continuity of consciousness is advanced from plane to plane, and fi-

---

[1] Bailey, Alice A., *Esoteric Psychology,* Vol. I, p. 370.

nally man achieves continuity of consciousness with monadic awareness. This is accomplished when the web between the second and third sub-planes of the Atmic Plane is burned away. This is how the Antahkarana is built. Man at this point is awake on all planes of his microcosm through which he works and serves.

The rending of webs does not guarantee the development of man nor the expansion of his consciousness if the rending is not caused by his steady achievement of spiritual realizations, by pure motives, inner striving, occult meditation, and a life of sacrificial service. These rents mean one thing to an average man, something else to a disciple, and something totally different to an Initiate. They are often caused by great explosions, radioactivity, drugs, breathing exercises, chanting, hatha yoga, loud music, and some special movements or dances.

When veils are rent, a new world emerges with new energies and new entities which dwell behind the veil. Initiates have a wonderful opportunity to come in contact with various planes, forces, and entities; to gather first hand knowledge, experience, and power to use the new energies. For an average man or a man on dark paths, these rents will cause trouble which will extend to his physical, emotional, and mental planes, leading him into depression and breakdowns or into a life of aimlessness, vanity, crime, and obsession.

It would be of great help if psychiatrists and psychologists would try to trace the causes of their patients' illnesses to the rending of veils and webs in their particular localities and within the individual mechanisms of the patients.

As we read occult literature, we are sometimes under the impression that the four lower ethers and the four higher ethers are the webs and veils. However, it seems to me that the ethers, lower and higher, and the veils or webs are of the same substance but that the veils and webs are formations within this substance of ether. For example, water, ice, and steam are of the same substance. Furthermore, I think we should make a distinction between veils and webs. We may say that veils are formed by human urges, desires, aspiration, thoughts, and actions, or even by the urges, desires, aspiration, thoughts, and actions of the Great Life "in Whom we live and move and have our being." These veils must be destroyed because they prevent unimpeded communication and unimpeded circulation of life energy among humanity, Hierarchy, Shamballa, and the far-off worlds.

Webs are diverse in nature. We may say that they are protective valves or gauges which open when the pressure in a given vehicle is too great. They serve to lessen the pressure and thus open a communication line between the inner and outer, or between limited and open space. They protect and make communication possible with the "higher." When the higher point of pressure is maintained, they act as doors between the "higher" and "lower" and are no longer obstructive.

We have similar etheric webs in the planetary Life itself. We are told that these webs are being built in a square pattern which is changing into a triangular one and eventually, as our planet enters into greater light, will become circular.

This transformation process is the best way to channel higher energies into lower planes for use in the progressive development of the sense of one humanity, one world, and to create a greater culture and greater civilization based on the sense of unity and synthesis.

In speaking of the war and the etheric web of the planet, the Tibetan Master says,

> *Through the power of prolonged sound, carried forward as a great experiment on the battlefields all over the world during a period of fours years (1914-1918), and through the intense emotional strain of the entire planetary populace, the web of etheric matter (called the "veil of the temple") which separates the physical and astral planes was rent or torn asunder, and the amazing process of unifying the two worlds of physical plane living and of astral plane experience was begun and is now slowly going on. It will be obvious, therefore, that this must bring about vast changes and alterations in the human consciousness. Whilst it will usher in the age of understanding, of brotherhood and of illumination, it will also bring about states of reaction and the letting loose of psychic forces which today menace the uncontrolled and ignorant, and warrant the sounding of a note of warning and of caution.*[1]

We are told that in the second part of the great war of 1939-1945 a larger rent was made in the etheric web of the planet because of the use of the atomic bomb. Master Djwhal Khul says,

---

[1] Bailey, Alice A., *The Externalisation of the Hierarchy*, p. 4.

> *... the release of atomic energy has had a far more potent effect in the etheric web than in the dense physical vehicle of the planet ... disrupting the etheric web ... and each time a great area of disruption was formed which will have future potent, and at present unsuspected, results.*[1]

We have no trouble seeing the results of these rents. We are aware that we have an in-rush of astral forces: lower psychism all over the world, especially in those areas where the web is rent; biological effects of radiation; a universal lack of control of sexual urges, of destructive and criminal drives with their dire consequences.

We also have emerging disciples who are entering into the path of greater responsibility, greater love, and greater sacrifice, unfolding within their nature higher psychic powers and serving one humanity with all that they have and are. We are told that Christ is using these rents to reach humanity, to lead humanity to the more abundant life.

Disciples and aspirants are invited to use an esoteric technique to help Christ in His great task of the redemption of the planet. This technique is the formation of a triangle by three people. They may be widely separated but linked together mentally and visualized as a triangle. At a certain chosen time of day, they recite simultaneously the *Great Invocation*. It must be said with deep aspiration, concentration, and meditation.

The Tibetan Master says that when such triangles increase all over the world, the destructive effects of the

---

[1] Bailey, Alice A., *Discipleship in the New Age*, Vol. II, p. 61.

rents will be offset and constructive energies will be evoked, assimilated, and expressed in spiritual creativity for the salvaging of humanity. Thus, instead of individual disciples working alone, groups of disciples will be working together to cause greater rents in the etheric webs. At the same time they will be carriers of benevolent energies from higher realms. This will lead us into a realization of the Hierarchy and the recognition of Its Head, the Christ.

To summarize this chapter we can say that three great Sons of God — Moses, Christ, and St. Paul — caused rents in the planetary veils. These rents were enlarged as a consequence of the great world war of 1914-1945, through the sounds on the battlefield, and through the explosion of atomic bombs. They were widened also by individual and group striving in service and meditation, which releases the fire of kundalini normally and causes minor or major rents.

Electricity has a great effect upon the rending of the veil between the astral and physical planes, and it releases a tremendous amount of light. The rending process is also carried on by some comets and by Cosmic Rays which pierce the veils and webs and bring in a great flood of new energy to the planet.

The greater, total rending of these three webs as well as of the fourth web will occur when Christ and Buddha together pass through the ceremony of the Seventh Initiation, thereby building a bridge connecting humanity, the Hierarchy, the Center where the Will of God is known, and Cosmos.

20

▲ CONTEMPORARY WORK OF THE CHRIST ▲

NOT LONG AGO one of the Masters of the Wisdom dictated twenty-four volumes of esoteric Teaching which are paving the way for one humanity; for joy, health and bliss; and especially for the externalization of the Hierarchy and for the reappearance of the Christ. In the following three chapters, I will mostly quote the fiery words of the Master referring to the contemporary work of Christ, His immediate task, and His future responsibilities.

The Master of Wisdom referred to is the Tibetan, or the Master Djwhal Khul. He has made profound statements about Christ and about His reappearance. He says that Christ is His Teacher and He calls Him

> *the Master of all Masters, and the Teacher alike of angels and men.*

He continues,

> *I am one who looks to the Christ as the supreme expression of divinity upon Earth....*

He further says that

> *He is the World Healer and Saviour ... the embodied soul of all Reality.*[1]

Speaking of Buddha and Christ He says,

> *Buddha ... revealed the process, but the Christ embodied in Himself both goal and process....*

Christ inaugurated

> *... the era wherein it became possible for the kingdom of God to appear on Earth.*[2]

> *The Buddha summed up in Himself all the light of the past as far as humanity was concerned. He was the culminating Messenger, and demonstrated the innate possibilities of mankind, radiating the light of wisdom in relation to the light of substance and producing that dual blaze or flaming light which had been fanned and fostered (though not fully expressed) by humanity up to that time. He came forth as the flower or fruition of the past and as the guarantee of man's innate capacity. Christ, whilst able also to say "I am the light of the world," went further in His manifestation and gave a vision of the*

---

[1] Bailey, Alice A., *Esoteric Healing*, p. 360.
[2] Bailey, Alice A., *Esoteric Astrology*, pp. 624-625.

next step, demonstrating the light of the soul and pointing to the future, thus presenting that which could be because He had released on Earth the cosmic principle of love. Love is an aspect of the will, which is a point very little realised by the mass of men. It is the will to draw into itself or the will to attract into itself, and this will, when exerted toward that which is not material, we, in reaction to the differentiating mind, call Love. But humanity has to see that which must be loved before that power of the will is sufficiently evoked. Then the vision can become a manifestation and a fact in expression.

... Christ ... makes it very clear that this love which He demonstrated was an aspect of the will, functioning through the medium of the second ray; this powerful love released into the world the cosmic principle of love.[1]

Further we are told that

... Christ put His disciples in touch with the "man, bearing a pitcher of water," Aquarius, and in the upper room introduced them to union and unity under the symbolism of the communion feast. For that feast, humanity is today preparing....[2]

It was the Buddha who clarified for man the nature of desire and its results, with the unhappy effects which desire produces when persistent and unenlightened. It was the Christ Who taught the transmutation of desire into aspiration which ... was

---

[1] Bailey, Alice A., *Esoteric Astrology*, pp. 623-624.
[2] *Ibid.*, pp. 167-168.

the effort of the human will (hitherto animated by, or expressed through, desire) to conform itself to the will of God — this without understanding but conformity, in perfect trust and with the inner assurance that the will of God must be all that is good, both in the individual and in the whole.[1]

Master Djwhal Khul says,

It might be of interest here to note that Christ was the first of our earth humanity to achieve the goal, whereas the Buddha was the last of the moon chain humanity to do so. As far as the development of these two sons of God was concerned, so rapid was the development of the Christ that in Atlantean days He found Himself upon the Path of Probation as did also the Buddha. He, coming into incarnation from the moon chain (having been held in ... "pralaya" till that time), entered upon the probationary Path a very short time ahead of His Brother, the Christ. From the angle of evolution the rapid unfoldment of the evolution of Christ was, and has been, totally unparalleled. *It has never been duplicated. ...*[2]

*... Christ, ... for the first time in planetary history, transmitted the cosmic energy of love di-*rectly *to the physical plane of our planet, and also in a peculiar manner to the fourth kingdom in nature, the human. This should indicate to you that though the love energy is the second aspect of divinity, the Christ embodied and transmitted four qualities of this*

---

[1] Bailey, Alice A., *Esoteric Astrology*, p. 371.
[2] Bailey, Alice A., *Esoteric Psychology*, Vol. II, p. 210.

> *aspect of humanity, and consequently to the other kingdoms in nature — the only four which humanity could absorb. Only one of these four is as yet beginning to express itself — the quality of goodwill. The other three will later be revealed, and one is related in a peculiar sense to the healing quality of love.*[1]

> *He, for the first time, presented the idea of the sacrifice of the unit, consciously and deliberately offered for the service of the whole.*[2]

Speaking about Christ's physical perfection the Tibetan Sage says,

> *All the seven centres in the etheric vehicle of the Christ were rightly adjusted, correctly aligned, truly awakened and functioning, and properly receptive of all the seven streams of energy coming from the seven planetary centres; these put Him en rapport, therefore, and in full realised contact, with the One in Whom He lived and moved and had His being . . . a perfect endocrine system. All His glands (both major and minor) were functioning correctly; this produced a "perfect man" — physically perfect, emotionally stable and mentally controlled . . . an expression of divine perfection to the entire world.*[3]

---

[1] Bailey, Alice A., *Esoteric Healing*, p. 616.
[2] *Ibid.*, p. 260.
[3] *Ibid.*, p. 621.

Further, the Tibetan Master gives very interesting information about the activities of Christ in the contemporary period. He says,

> ...*The Lord Maitreya with His workers is approaching nearer all the time to the physical plane. The focus of His attention in the year 1936 was, for the first time, predominantly on the first subplane of the astral plane. Hence the sensitives' correct and immediate response to His energy there expressed. He is coming nearer in His thought and activity. Should the peoples of the world respond to the presented opportunity, His forces and attention could penetrate more deeply and be predominantly on etheric levels with all that is implied in such a situation.*
>
> *This, many sense subjectively and know; and great, therefore, is their opportunity and yours to constitute increasingly a channel for this force.*
>
> *Remember that the work for which He comes and to which the attendant Hierarchy is pledged is to help Him in the "healing of the nations" as it is expressed in the Bible.... This healing will be brought about if men of goodwill everywhere measure up to their opportunity; if the work of the Christ and of His helpers is brought more definitely to the attention of the general public....*[1]

Giving some astrological information the Master says,

---

[1] Bailey, Alice A., *Esoteric Healing*, pp. 361-362.

> *In Scorpio* — Hercules became the triumphant disciple.
> *In Taurus* — The Buddha achieved victory over desire and arrived at illumination.
> *In Pisces* — The Christ overcame death and became the world saviour.[1]

We are told that in 1936 Christ gave us the first stanza of the *Great Invocation*. In 1940 He gave us the second stanza. And in 1945, at the June full moon, He gave the third stanza of the *Great Invocation*, which in very short time became a world prayer translated into more than one hundred and twenty languages. Here are the three stanzas, and we are told that He will give us the fourth one.

THE GREAT INVOCATION

Stanza One (1935)

*Let the Forces of Light bring illumination
  to mankind.
Let the Spirit of Peace be spread abroad.
May men of goodwill everywhere meet in
  a spirit of cooperation.
May forgiveness on the part of all men be
  the keynote at this time.
Let power attend the efforts of the Great Ones.
So let it be, and help us to do our part.*

---

[1] Bailey, Alice A., *Esoteric Astrology*, p. 204.

Stanza Two (1940)

Let the Lords of Liberation issue forth.
Let Them bring succour to the sons of men.
Let the Rider from the Secret Place come forth,
And coming, save.
Come forth, O Mighty One.

Let the souls of men awaken to the Light,
And may they stand with massed intent.
Let the fiat of the Lord go forth:
The end of woe has come!
The hour of service of the
    Saving Force has now arrived.
Let it be spread abroad, O Mighty One.

Let Light and Love and Power and Death
Fulfill the purpose of the Coming One.
The WILL to save is here.
The LOVE to carry forth the work is
    widely spread abroad.
The ACTIVE AID of all who know the truth
    is also here.
Come forth, O Mighty One and blend these three.
Construct a great defending wall.
The rule of evil now must end.

Stanza Three (1945)

From the point of Light within the Mind of God
Let light stream forth into the minds of men.
Let Light descend on Earth.

*From the point of Love within the Heart of God
Let love stream forth into the hearts of men.
May Christ return to Earth.*

*From the centre where the Will of God is known
Let purpose guide the little wills of men —
The purpose which the Masters know and serve.*

*From the centre which we call the race of men
Let the Plan of Love and Light work out.
And may it seal the door where evil dwells.*

*Let Light and Love and Power
restore the Plan on Earth.*[1]

Writing to His disciples in December, 1941, the Tibetan Sage said,

> *The determination and the inner purpose of humanity will be so definite during the period when the Sun will begin to move northward — from December 25th until June 22nd, 1942 — that the future of humanity for many hundreds of years will be decided. From that decision will date the coming New Age; on that decision, the Hierarchy will be able to make prediction and determine action....*[2]

We are told that in 1942 the tide was shifted to the forces of Light, and from the full moon of May 30th to June 15th, 1942, the forces of Shamballa were released and a terrific onslaught was carried on, especially against

---

[1] Bailey, Alice A., *The Externalisation of the Hierarchy*, p. v.
[2] *Ibid.*, p. 337.

the powers of evil. The student of history will find profound hints in this information. In 1944 Christ and Buddha, joining Their powers, shifted the Shamballa force back to the center of Love, to the Hierarchy.

In His full moon message of June, 1944, the Tibetan Master wrote,

> *At the time of the June Full Moon, each year, the love of God, the spiritual essence of solar fire, reaches its highest point of expression. . . . The Full Moon of June 1943 saw this outpouring of divine love reach its highest expression for all time. . . .*
> *The love of God, focussed in the Christ, seeks to express itself in some act of peculiarly useful service to humanity.*[1]
>
> *Today the Hierarchy is facing a climaxing activity. From the Full Moon of May, 1944, until the Full Moon of May, 1945, the Members of the Hierarchy will unitedly be putting forth Their maximum effort to close the door upon the Forces of Evil. . . .*[2] (Written in May, 1944.)

This was how the war came to an end!

In June of 1945 Christ promised the Hierarchy to remain with humanity another great cycle, 2500 years, and to reappear in His physical appearance.

---

[1] Bailey, Alice A., *The Rays and the Initiations*, pp. 88-89.
[2] Bailey, Alice A., *The Externalisation of the Hierarchy*, p. 437.

> *At the time of the Full Moon of April 1945, during the Easter season of that year and covering approximately a period of five weeks, the Forces of Restoration began their work, emerging first upon the subtler planes of human experience. This type of energy is peculiarly creative in nature and carries the "life which produces the birth of forms." ...*
>
> *... At the time of the Full Moon of the Buddha in May 1945, the forces of enlightenment became active, and light began to stream into the minds of men. These are, in reality, the energies which initiate the new world education. ...*
>
> *In June 1945, Christ set in motion the forces of reconstruction which are related to the Will aspect of divinity. ... The main object of the Hierarchy is so to distribute these constructive, synthesising energies that the theory of unity may slowly be turned into practice, and the word "United" may come to have a true significance and meaning.*[1]

On August 9, 1945, the Tibetan Master issued an instruction about the release of atomic energy in which He said,

> *This world war started in 1914, but its last and most important phase began in 1939. Up till then it was a world war. After that date, and because the forces of evil took advantage of the state of war and belligerency existing on the planet, the real war began, involving the entire three worlds of human*

---

[1] Bailey, Alice A., *The Reappearance of the Christ*, pp. 90-93.

evolution and a consequent activity of the Hierarchy.[1]

... The evil forces were closer to success than any of you have ever dreamed. They were so close to success in 1942 that there were four months when the members of the spiritual Hierarchy had made every possible arrangement to withdraw from human contact for an indefinite and unforeseen period of time; the plans for a closer contact with the evolutionary process in the three worlds and the effort to blend and fuse the two divine centres, the Hierarchy and Humanity, into one working, collaborating whole seemed doomed to destruction.

... The Lords of Liberation took certain unexpected steps. This They were led to do owing to the invocative powers of humanity, used consciously by all those upon the side of the will-to-good and unconsciously by all men of goodwill. Owing to these steps, the efforts of those fighting in the realm of science for the establishing of true knowledge and right human relations were aided. The trend of the power to know and to discover ... was deflected away from the demanding evocative minds of those seeking to destroy the world of men, leading to a form of mental paralysis. Those seeking to emphasise the right values and to save humanity were simultaneously stimulated to the point of success.

---

[1] Bailey, Alice A., *The Externalisation of the Hierarchy*, pp. 491-492.

... When the Sun moved northward that year (1942), the Great White Lodge knew that the battle had been won.[1]

Speaking about the return of Christ, the Tibetan Master says,

... The "point of decision," as it is called in all hierarchical circles, was reached during the period between the Full Moon of June, 1936, and the Full Moon of June, 1945. The point of decision covered, therefore, nine years... ; it resulted in the decision arrived at by the Christ to re-appear or return to visible Presence on Earth as soon as possible, and considerably earlier than had been planned.

This decision was necessarily made in consultation with the Lord of the World, the "Ancient of Days.".... [2]

Speaking of some Cosmic Beings Who came to help Christ with His great responsibility, the Tibetan Sage says,

Whilst this energy has been accumulating or mounting in potency ever since the Full Moon of June 1945, three events of great moment in the living experience of Christ... have taken place....

1. The Spirit of Peace *descended upon Christ....*

---

[1] Bailey, Alice A., *The Externalisation of The Hierarchy*, pp. 493-494.
[2] Bailey, Alice A., *The Reappearance of the Christ*, p. 69.

2. The evolutionary force ... focussed itself in the person of the Christ in a manner hitherto unknown. ...

3. ... As a result of Christ's decision and His "spiritual fusion" with the Will of God, the Avatar of Synthesis [a great Cosmic Entity] has become, for the time being, His close Associate. ... His relationship and planned help date from the time of the pronouncing of the great Invocation and its use by men everywhere. Owing to the stupendous task confronting Christ, the Avatar of Synthesis will fortify Him, and He will be buttressed by this "Silent Avatar" Who (to speak symbolically) will "keep His eye upon Him, His hand beneath Him and His heart in unison with His."[1]

In June, 1945, at the time of the full moon ..., He definitely and consciously took over His duties and responsibilities as the Teacher and Leader during the Aquarian solar cycle. He is the first of the great world Teachers to cover two zodiacal cycles — the Piscean and the Aquarian. ... His outpouring love and spiritual vitality (augmented by the energies of the Spirit of Peace, the Avatar of Synthesis and the Buddha) were refocussed and channelled into a great stream, pulled through into expression ... by the words of the Invocation, "Let love stream forth into the hearts of men. ... Let Light and Love and Power restore the Plan on Earth."

---

[1] Bailey, Alice A., *The Reappearance of the Christ*, pp. 73-77.

In those three words — light, love and power — the energies of His three Associates (the great Triangle of Force which stands in power behind Him) are described: the energy of the Buddha: Light, for the light ever comes from the East; the energy of the Spirit of Peace: Love, establishing right human relations; the energy of the Avatar of Synthesis: Power, implementing both light and love. At the centre of this Triangle the Christ took His stand; from that point His Aquarian work began, and it will continue for two thousand five hundred years. Thus He inaugurated the new era and, upon the inner spiritual planes, the new world religion began to take form.[1]

---

[1] Bailey, Alice A., *The Reappearance of the Christ*, pp. 82-83.

21

▲ THE CHRIST TODAY ▲

Lo, I am with you all the days, even unto the end of the world.[1]

Khalki-Avatara will be endowed with the eight superhuman faculties. By His irresistible power He will overthrow all the evil-motivated people, and the thieves, and all those whose minds are devoted to iniquity.

Then he will re-establish right doing on earth, and the minds of them who live at the end of the Kali-Yuga shall be as pellucid as crystal. The men thus changed by the influence of that exceptional period shall be the seeds of human beings to come, and shall grow into a Race which will follow the duties and Laws of the Age of purity.[2]

---

[1] Matthew 28:20
[2] *Vishnu Purana*, Book IV, Ch. 24.

In occult literature, especially in the Teachings of Blavatsky, Master Morya, and Djwhal Khul, Christ is a living Being involved in human affairs, sensitive to human needs, sensitive to the sorrows, sufferings, and joys of humanity. He looks upon humanity as one family and tries to help every nation grow and establish right human relations with one another in order to reach eventually the state of World Brotherhood.

A vision and a plan for humanity exist and for each human being. The achievements of Christ unveiled to us that plan and that vision.

All countries, with their cultures and civilizations, were directed to create a Christ, the model of the vision for humanity. He was the One from our humanity Who for the first time achieved the highest perfection. That was why He was given the sole authority to teach about the Plan of God and about the Purpose of God. In the *New Testament* He Himself said that there is only one Teacher, the Christ. When He comes back and further unveils His nature, we will see that He is the goal toward which all humanity is oriented.

In every human being there exists the stupendous urge toward perfection, toward conscious immortality, toward freedom from ignorance, disease, old-age, and death.

Christ is there as One Who has achieved all human hopes and can say, "Be courageous. I overcometh the world." He is

> ... *the World Teacher.* ... *He is that Great Being Whom the Christian calls the Christ; He is known also in the Orient as the Bodhisattva, and as the Lord Maitreya, and is the One looked for by the devout Mohammedan, under the name of the Iman*

▲ THE CHRIST TODAY ▲ 199

Madhi . . . and to Him is committed the guidance of the spiritual destinies of men, and the development of the realisation within each human being that he is a child of God and a son of the Most High.[1]

. . . Ever since He left the earth . . . has He stayed with the sons of men; never has He really gone, but only in appearance, and in a physical body He can be found by those who know the way, dwelling in the Himalayas, and working in close cooperation with His two great Brothers, the Manu and the Mahachohan [The Lord of Civilisation]. Daily He pours out His blessing on the world, and daily He stands under the great pine in His garden at the sunset hour with hands uplifted in blessing over all those who truly and earnestly seek to aspire.[2]

. . . The Christ, as the Leader of the Forces of Light, has empowered the Ashrams of the Masters upon this first Ray of Power to strengthen the hands of all disciples in the field of government and of political arrangement in every nation; to enlighten, if possible, the various national legislatures by whatever means may be needed, so that the potency of their words, the wisdom of their planning, and the breadth of their thinking may prove so effective that the "Cycle of Conferences and of Councils," now being initiated by the statesmen of the world, may be under the direct guidance . . . of Those in the

---

[1] Bailey, Alice A., *Initiation, Human and Solar*, pp. 43-44.
[2] *Ibid.*, p. 44.

Council Chamber at Shamballa Who know what is the Will of God.[1]

Skill in action, wise and understanding judgment, the adaptation of present affairs to the desired future, the coordination of the work to be done, and the clear enunciation of the platform upon which the new teaching must be founded, plus the survey . . . of the foundations upon which the new structure of the coming civilisation must be founded — it is with these things that the Christ is at this time concerned.[2]

The Spirit of Christ breathes across the desert of life.
Like a spring It wears Its way through the solid rocks.
In the milky firmament It radiates in myriads of lights, and rises upward in the stems of flowers.[3]

. . . Maitreya is coming, radiant with all fires. His Heart flames with compassion for destitute humanity. His Heart flames with the affirmation of the new Covenants.[4]

In order to make this possible and thus release His spiritual Brother [Buddha] *from the arduous task of relating humanity to the "centre where the will of God is known" (Shamballa), Christ is subjecting Himself at this time to an unique process of training. . . . The lines which His training follows are*

---

[1] Bailey, Alice A., *The Externalisation of the Hierarchy*, p. 446.
[2] *Ibid.*, p. 662.
[3] Agni Yoga Society, *Leaves of Morya's Garden*, Vol. I, para. 72.
[4] Agni Yoga Society, *Hierarchy*, para. 3.

> known only to Christ, to the Buddha and to the Avatar of Synthesis.[1]

We are told that above the Gobi Desert, in the second ether, there is a great center of energies which is called Shamballa, or the Head Center of the planet, through which issues the directing Will of our Planetary Logos. Only very high Initiates have permission to enter there, attend the great Council, and be instructed in the Will of God.

We are told that Christ is a member of the Shamballa Center and that He occasionally attends meetings there. It is very interesting to know also that He has a Rod of Power about which the following information is given:

> *In the sceptre of a ruling monarch at this day is hidden the symbolism of these various Rods. They are duly recognised as symbols of office and of power, but it is not generally appreciated that they are of electrical origin, and that their true significance is concerned with the dynamic stimulation of all the subordinates in office who come under their touch, thus inspiring them to increased activity and service for the race.*
>
> *The great Rod of Power of the Logos Himself is hidden in the sun. . . .*
>
> 1. *The Rod of the Bodhisattva* [Christ] *lies hidden in the "heart of the wisdom," that is, at Shamballa.*
> 2. *The Rod of the One Initiator is hidden in "the East," a definite planetary location.*

---

[1] Bailey, Alice A., *The Reappearance of the Christ*, pp. 97, 99.

> 3. *The Rod of the solar Logos is hidden in "the heart of the sun," that mysterious subjective sphere which lies back of our physical sun, and of which our physical sun is but the environing shield and envelope.*
> 4. *The Rod of the cosmic Logos associated with our solar Logos is secreted in that central spot in the heavens around which our solar system revolves, and which is termed "the central spiritual sun."* [1]
>
> *One Rod of Initiation is used for the first two initiations, and is wielded by the Great Lord. It is magnetised by the application of the "Flaming Diamond," the magnetisation being repeated for each new World Teacher. There is a wonderful ceremony performed at the time that a new World Teacher takes office, in which He receives His Rod of Power — the same Rod as used since the foundation of our Planetary Hierarchy — and holds it forth to the Lord of the World, Who touches it with His own mighty Rod, causing a fresh recharging of its electric capacity. This ceremony takes place at Shamballa.*[2]

Christ uses this Rod on various occasions, for example, at the time of the first two initiations. Also, He uses it at the time of the Wesak Ceremony.[3] In using the Rod, He transmits energy through which He purifies, charges, and bridges certain centers in the initiate and in the planet.

---

[1] Bailey, Alice A., *Initiation, Human and Solar,* pp. 129-130.
[2] *Ibid.*, pp. 128-129.
[3] See *The Science of Meditation* by Torkom Saraydarian, pp. 349-358.

22

▲ CHRIST IN THE IMMEDIATE FUTURE ▲

...*When we approach the ominous hour, all forces must be strained for the mighty step. It has already been told that the Epoch of Maitreya is approaching and the signs are strewn as fiery seeds; hence, the ominous hour will be one of Light for those who are in step with the Cosmic Magnet. Hence, the ominous hour will be as a future Light for those who battle for the significance of the Epoch of Maitreya. Hence, cooperation with Us brings the predestined victory. Therefore, the co-workers who walk in self-denial will be victors. Proceeding in step with the Cosmic Magnet, you affirm victory! Yes, yes, yes!*[1]

---

[1] Agni Yoga Society, *Infinity*, Vol. II, para. 55.

> ...*In symbolic form, the legend runs that when the Buddha reached enlightenment, and experience on Earth could teach Him no more, He looked ahead to the time when His Brother, the Christ, would be active in the Great Service — as it is called. In order, therefore, to aid the Christ, He left behind Him (for His use) what are mysteriously called "His vestures." He bequeathed and left in some safe place the sumtotal of His emotional-intuitive nature, called by some the astral body and the sumtotal of His knowledge and His thought, called His mind or mental body. These, the legend says, will be assumed by the Coming One and prove of service, supplementing Christ's Own emotional and mental equipment and providing Him with what He needs as the Teacher of the East as well as of the West.*[1]

The same legend is repeated in *A Treatise on Cosmic Fire*, adding more information.

> *The vestures act in a dual capacity:*
>
> a. *They are very highly magnetised, and therefore have a profound and far-reaching effect when utilised.*
> b. *They act as a focal point for the force of the Lord Buddha and link up the coming Lord with Him, enabling Him to increase His Own stupendous resources by drawing upon still higher force*

---

[1] Bailey, Alice A., *The Reappearance of the Christ*, pp. 100-101.

centres, via the Lord Buddha.[1]

It might be of interest here to point out that when He comes Whom angels and men await, and Whose work it is to inaugurate the new age and so complete the work He began in Palestine two thousand years ago, He will bring with Him some of the great Angels, as well as certain of the Masters. . . .

These four groups of angels are a band of servers, pledged to the service of the Christ, and their work is to contact men and to teach them along certain lines.

a. *They will teach humanity to see etherically. . . .*
b. *They will give instruction in the effect of colour in the healing of disease, and particularly the efficiency of violet light in lessening human ills and in curing those physical plane sicknesses which originate in the etheric body.*
c. *They will also demonstrate to the materialistic thinkers of the world the fact that the superconscious world exists and that angels and men who are out of incarnation and possess no physical bodies can be contacted and known.*
d. *They will train human beings in the knowledge of superhuman physics so that weight shall be for them transmuted. Motion will become more rapid, speed will be accompanied by noiseless-*

---

[1] Bailey, Alice A., *A Treatise on Cosmic Fire*, p. 754. Also see pp. 1192-1193; and Blavatsky, H.P., *The Voice of the Silence*, pp. 97-98.

ness and smoothness, and hence fatigue will be eliminated. . . .

e. *They will teach humanity how rightly to nourish the body and to draw from the surrounding ethers the requisite food.*[1]

. . . *His [Christ's] reappearance will knit and bind together all men and women of goodwill throughout the world, irrespective of religion or nationality. His coming will evoke among men a widespread and mutual recognition of the good in all.*[2]

. . . *He will not come alone but will be accompanied by Those Whose lives and words will evoke recognition in every department of human thinking.*[3]

. . . *From the quiet mountain retreat where He has waited, guided and watched over humanity and where He has trained His disciples, initiates and the New Group of World Servers, He must come forth and take His place prominently on the world stage.*[4]

. . . *All who knew Him in earlier incarnations in the ancient East, all whom He cured or taught, all who contacted Him or in any way incurred*

---

[1] Bailey, Alice A., *The Externalisation of the Hierarchy*, pp. 508-509.
[2] Bailey, Alice A., *The Reappearance of the Christ*, pp. 21-22.
[3] *Ibid.*, p. 45.
[4] *Ibid.*, pp. 54-55.

> *karma with Him or with the Master Jesus, will have the opportunity to cooperate at this time.*[1]

> *... When the Great One comes with His disciples and initiates we shall have ... the restoration of the Mysteries and their exoteric presentation, as a consequence of the first initiation. Why can this be so? Because the Christ ... is the Hierophant of the first and second initiations. ...*[2]

In the Tibetan's books there are references about Masters Who are working for the reappearance of Christ: Master Morya, the Rajput Prince, the Chohan of the First Ray; the Master Koot Hoomi, the great Master Who is going to replace Christ after 2500 years and be the Christ of humanity, the Head of the Hierarchy; Master Jesus; Master Hilarion; Master Djwhal Khul; the Master of India; one of the English Masters; the Lord of Civilization, the Master R.; two Masters in America; and others whose names are not made public.

In *The Reappearance of the Christ* the Master Djwhal Khul summarizes the work Christ is going to do when He reappears. He is going to establish **right human relations.** *The Externalisation of the Hierarchy* continues:

> *The main objective and the immediate task of the Christ is to bring to an end the separateness which*

---

[1] Bailey, Alice A., *The Externalisation of the Hierarchy*, p. 514.
[2] *Ibid.*, pp. 514-515.

exists between man and man, family and family, community and community, and nation and nation.[1]

... The bringing in of the Kingdom of God, the preparation for the coming of the Christ and the salvaging of mankind demand courage, organisation, business acumen, psychology and persistence; it needs trained workers and much money; it calls for the carefully considered programmes, possessing long range vision, plus sensible modern procedures.[2]

He will teach the **law of rebirth**, and the Tibetan Master says that

... in the recognition of this law will be found the solution of all problems of humanity, and the answer to much of human questioning.[3]

He will reveal the **mysteries of initiation**.

These ancient Mysteries were originally given to humanity by the Hierarchy and contain the entire clue to the evolutionary process, hidden in numbers, in ritual, in words and in symbology; these veil the secret of man's origin and destiny, picturing to him, in rite and ritual, the long, long path which he must tread, back into the light.[4]

He will dispel **glamor**.

---

[1] Bailey, Alice A., *The Externalisation of the Hierarchy*, p. 648.
[2] *Ibid.*, pp. 650-651.
[3] Bailey, Alice A., *The Reappearance of the Christ*, p. 116.
[4] *Ibid.*, p. 122.

> *...The greatest service a man can render his fellow men is to free himself from the control of that* [astral] *plane by himself directing its energies through the power of the Christ within. . . . Christ is the great dispeller of world glamour when He comes, and in this work the Buddha has previously prepared the way.*[1]

In the wisdom of the esoteric Teaching we are told that there are four great obstacles on the path of the aspirant and of humanity. The first one is called *glamor*, the second one is *illusion*, the third one is *maya*, and the fourth one is called the *Dweller on the Threshold*.[2]

Glamors are like post-hypnotic suggestions in our emotional sphere. When things attract us and when we extend ourselves to the object of desire and identify with it, in some degree, we form a glamor. We build or attract glamors when we are in need, in despair, hurt, or in painful emotions. We call them emotional "hang-ups" or attachments. All these create an unhealthy condition around our body, preventing us from receiving true light, true understanding, and seeing things as they are.

Glamors are contagious. Our glamors can be projected to others and cause infection. Glamors may be in space, and we can draw them into ourselves if we contact them through our fears, hatreds, and angers. These three negative emotions open channels in our aura to absorb related glamors and become infected by them. The greatest protection from infection is again faith,

---

[1] Bailey, Alice A., *The Reappearance of the Christ*, pp. 130-132.
[2] Read *The Science of Meditation* by Torkom Saraydarian, pp. 279-291.

love, and hope. These create positive attitudes in us and repel the glamors.

In *The Science of Meditation* it was written that glamor is formed by "correct registration of illusive phenomena which is taken or accepted as a part of reality by the unfolding human soul, identified with the astral and physical body."[1]

The *glamor of sex* is a big glamor. Let us see how it is formed. When one sees a picture of a kiss or of lovemaking or of a naked body, the image is impressed upon his mind. Immediately after it is impressed, his past pleasures, habits, and associations gather themselves around that impression and make it grow like a snowball. Eventually it becomes a powerful, dominating, crystallized factor in his astral aura.

Glamor grows as we feed it through our imagination and frequent opportunities to satisfy its urges. It becomes dominant and uses all our interests for its own growth. For example, our business relations, our school relations, our choice of a house or furniture or vacations or art — whatever we do is motivated by our sex glamor. This glamor does not stay in our aura; it duplicates and reinforces itself in the aura of others with whom we have a relationship. Thus, from man to man it grows and forms a terrible, overshadowing glamor which controls our life on physical, astral, and mental levels. This is the case throughout the world.

In childhood we slept on and nursed at the breasts of our mothers. We enjoyed the milk and got our life, joy, and nourishment from the love of our mother. The memory of a very beautiful experience remains waiting

---

[1] Saraydarian, Torkom, *The Science of Meditation*, p. 280.

in our mind to make us be attracted to a girl's breasts and awaken all our former sensations and associations with females.

Here you have also a very deep and mysterious registration. For example, after you were conceived your daddy probably made love with your mother, and every time he pressed upon you, you felt uncomfortable and were more ready to be impressed by the words of your mother, father and the sensations of both. In this way, a great preconditioning factor was prepared in your emotional nature which at any time could contribute to any future experience and turn it into a glamor.

How can this be controlled? Freud suggested that it could be controlled by exposing it. This was a great failure because all his suggestions were immediately used by our sex glamor and became the cause of greater license and waste of energy — which created worse sicknesses in the human being.

Others suggested that it is better to suppress that glamor and not allow it to express itself. This was another error.

The Ageless Wisdom teaches

1. That you must observe yourself and find out why you act a certain way. This is the process of knowing yourself.
2. When you recognize your glamor, analyze it in the light of the Soul, not in your emotional and lower mental "reasoning." Then focus your Soul-illumined light upon your glamor and try to make it evaporate or disintegrate. Soon you will see that you are no longer controlled by any outer pictures or thoughtforms. When you find a

glamor, try to see how it was formed and how it is controlling you and your relations with others.

The Soul in man is the inner Christ. Through the power of the inner Christ, the glamors must be dispelled. Humanity has many global glamors which obscure its vision and form thick veils between the true values of life and humanity. It is the Christ Who will help us eliminate these glamors and "see things as they are." The approach of the Christ is gradually forming the New World Religion. The Tibetan Master says that the New World Religion will have three Major Festivals each year:

> ... *These three festivals are concentrated in three consecutive months and lead, therefore, to a prolonged annual spiritual effort which should affect the entire year.* ...
>
> *1. The Festival of Easter. This is the festival of the risen, living Christ, the Head of the spiritual Hierarchy, the Inaugurator of the Kingdom of God and the Expression of the love of God. On this day, the spiritual Hierarchy which He guides and directs will be universally recognized, man's relation to it emphasized and the nature of God's love registered. Men everywhere will invoke that love, with its power to produce resurrection and spiritual livingness. This Festival is determined always by the date of the first Full Moon of spring. The eyes and thoughts of men will be fixed on life, not death; Good Friday will no longer be a factor in the life of the churches. Easter will be the great Western festival.*

II. The Festival of Wesak or Vaisakha. *This is the festival of the Buddha, that great spiritual Intermediary between the center where the will of God is known and the spiritual Hierarchy. The Buddha is the expression of the will of God, the embodiment of Light and the indicator of the divine purpose. Men everywhere will evoke wisdom and understanding and the inflow of light into the minds of men everywhere. This Festival is determined in relation to the Full Moon of Taurus. It is the great Eastern festival and is already meeting with Western recognition; thousands of Christians today keep the festival of the Buddha.*

III. The Festival of Humanity. *This will be the festival of the spirit of humanity — aspiring to approach nearer to God, seeking conformity to the divine will to which the Buddha called attention, dedicated to the expression of goodwill which is the lowest aspect of love to which Christ called attention and of which He was the perfect expression. It will be the day preeminently on which the divine nature of man will be recognized and his power to express goodwill and to establish right human relations (because of his divinity) will be stressed. On this festival we are told Christ has for nearly two thousand years represented humanity and has stood before the Hierarchy as the God-man, the leader of His people and "the Eldest in a great family of brothers." This will, therefore, be a festival of deep invocation and appeal; it will express a basic aspiration toward fellowship and for human and spiritual unity; it will represent the effect in the human consciousness of the work of the Buddha and of the Christ. It will be held at the time of the Full Moon of Gemini.*

If in these early days of restoration and of the inauguration of the new civilization and of the new world, men of all faiths and all religions, of every cult and all esoteric groups were to keep these three great Festivals of Invocation, simultaneously and with understanding of the far-reaching implications, a great spiritual unity would be achieved; if they unitedly invoked the spiritual Hierarchy and sought consciously to contact its Head a great and general inflow of spiritual light and love would occur; if they together determined, with steadfastness and understanding, to approach nearer to God, who could doubt the stupendous results which eventually would be seen? Not only would an underlying unity between men of all faiths be attained, not only would brotherhood be recognized as a fact and not only would our oneness of origin, of goal and of life be recognized but that which would be evoked would change all aspects of human living, would condition our civilization, change our mode of life and make the spiritual world a dominant reality in the human consciousness.

God, in the person of Christ and His Hierarchy, would draw nearer to His people; God, through the instrumentality of the Buddha, would reveal His eternal light and evoke our intelligent cooperation; God, through the spiritual Hierarchy and through that center where the will of God is known, would bring humanity to the point of resurrection and to a spiritual awareness which would bring about goodwill toward men and peace on earth. The will of

God transcendent would be carried out through the medium of God immanent in man; it would be expressed in love in response to the work of Christ; it would be intelligently presented on earth because the minds of men would have been illumined as the result of their united invocation, the unity of their effort and the oneness of their understanding.

It is for this that humanity waits; it is for this that the churches must work; it is these qualities and characteristics which will condition the New World Religion.

The great Invocation or Prayer does not belong to any person or group but to all Humanity. The beauty and the strength of this Invocation lies in its simplicity, and in its expression of certain central truths which all men, innately and normally, accept — the truth of the existence of a basic Intelligence to Whom we vaguely give the name of God; the truth that behind all outer seeming, the motivating power of the universe is Love; the truth that a great Individuality came to earth, called by Christians, the Christ, and embodied that love so that we could understand; the truth that both love and intelligence are effects of what is called the Will of God; and finally the self-evident truth that only through humanity *itself can the Divine Plan work out.*[1]

... The appearance of the Great Lord on the astral plane (whether followed by His physical incarnation or not) will date from a certain Wesak festival at which a mantram (known only to those attaining

---

[1] Bailey, Alice A., *Problems of Humanity*, pp. 163-166.

the seventh Initiation) will be pronounced by the Buddha, thus setting loose force, and enabling His great Brother to fulfil his mission. ...

When the hour strikes (five years prior to the date of His descent) they [the present children] *will be in the full flower of their service and will have recognised their work, even though they may not be conscious of that which the future holds hid.*

When the hour has come..., many cases of overshadowing *will be seen.... In all countries, in the orient and the occident, prepared disciples and highly evolved men and women, will be found who will be doing the work along the lines intended and who will be occupying places of prominence which will make them available for the reaching of the many; their bodies also will be sufficiently pure to permit of the overshadowing. It will only be possible in the case of those who have been consecrated since childhood, who have been servers of the race all their lives, or who, in previous lives, have acquired the right by karma.*[1]

---

[1] Bailey, Alice A., *A Treatise on Cosmic Fire*, p. 756.

23

▲ THE WAY TO CHRIST ▲

THERE IS A TECHNIQUE by which we can contact the great Individual Whom we call Christ. It is the technique of occult meditation.

It is through meditation that the bridge of communication is built between the unfolding human soul and the Inner Guide, the transpersonal Self. Upon this bridge the consciousness of the human being is expanded to such a degree that the impressions coming from Christ are contacted, His radiations are registered, His Plan is recognized, and His call is answered. The response to His call is a lifelong sacrificial service to His Plan for humanity.

Meditation is an inexhaustible subject. It is like a big tree; it is so branched out that if you want to talk about meditation, you cannot talk about the whole subject. You must talk about one branch, two, three, or four branches, and when you find that you have discussed all the branches — next spring you will see that new branches are emerging. All these branches, all these aspects of meditation have one common denominator which I call the total transformation of the human being. The goal of meditation is the total transformation of the human being — transformation of our physical body, transformation of our emotional reactions, transformation of our mind, and then a total down-flow of energy of inspiration and enlightenment which is the prelude to contact with the Jewel of all ages.

This transformation takes place in the following manner. At the time of true meditation — scientific meditation — the lower energies orient themselves upward; higher energies are evoked and they descend. When these energies meet on the mental plane, a great fusion commences: two energies blend into one another causing sublimation.

For example, we have physical energy, energies of the etheric body. The entire energy system of the physical body is based on the seven etheric centers: head center, ajna center, throat center, heart center, solar plexus, sex center, and kundalini center. These seven centers condition the etheric body's energy system. We also have emotional centers which are the counterparts of these etheric or physical centers. Then we have four mental centers. These are the lower forces which are going to be oriented and polarized toward the higher mind. How does that polarization come about? It is an esoteric fact that *wherever our consciousness is focused, there the energies flow*. For example, when you think about the physical body, energies flow to the physical body. When you think about your emotions, energies flow to your emotional system. If you think on the mental level and concentrate or focus your consciousness on the mental plane, you raise the energies to the mental plane.

The flow of energy is conditioned by your mental activity or by the focus of your consciousness. If your consciousness is focused on the sex center, all your emotional and mental energies flow in that direction. If the focus of your consciousness is on the object of your hatred, all your physical and mental energies concentrate on satisfying your hatred. If your entire consciousness is focused on your mental problems, your physical and emotional energies work as fuel to force your mental body to achieve its goal. When you meditate you are actually orienting and focusing these energies upon the mental plane. This is why deep thinkers are totally oriented, physically and emotionally, toward their mental visions. Deep thinkers do not extend their energies to different aspects of their nature, especially at times of drastic activities.

Thus, at the time of meditation, the lower forces are oriented upward toward the mental plane, and, by the power of resonance, by the power of the law of frequencies, the higher counterparts of these energies are evoked from the higher realms. For example, we have a triangle called Light, Wisdom, and Power present in the higher mind, Intuitional Plane, and Atmic Plane. These latter three are reflected in our physical, emotional, and mental bodies. In meditation, these higher energies — the Light, the Intuition and the Spiritual Will — are coming in contact with the force field of our physical brain, nervous system and the glands, emotional body, and mental body. This contact is creating a fusion between two natures — the higher and lower — and the lower nature is entering into a process of transmutation and transfiguration, a process accomplished by deep thinking. We are told that the mind is fiery in nature; it is the field upon which the transformation process takes place. Thinking is a burning process in which the lower nature is undergoing a change and the power of the higher nature is penetrating the lower vehicles. Thinking is the ignition; it is like bringing fire in contact with charcoal, causing it to burn.

On the physical plane, meditation can cause healing, purification, and energizing. To the emotional nature, it may bring peace, positiveness, and magnetism. To the mental nature, it provides the answers to many questions, meets the needs of the whole personality, and lessens the karma.

Man's entire nature is affected by meditation. The cells and atoms receive greater light; they become more receptive and more sensitive to higher energies; a greater integration and alignment come into play; and, eventually, the whole personality becomes fused and blended with the light, intuitional, and will energies. Meditation is a process of asking and receiving, invoking and evoking; it is taking and giving; it is a continuous act of absorbing and penetrating. It brings the mental nature together and organizes it highly.

An unorganized mind loses its sensitivity, its discriminative power, and day after day it creates greater problems upon its own path. As these problems increase, the mind loses its sanity, causing great complications in its physical and emotional equipment. In the presence of people with unorganized minds, you feel great tension, irritation, and eventually loss of energy. Their minds are chaotic and from them emanates very distressing ultrasonic noise. This noise affects your aura by causing a temporary or lasting disturbance.

These effects must be cleaned by daily meditation. Meditation not only cleans these disturbances but also fortifies your aura. Eventually it builds a shield of protection with a high level frequency of vibration which repels all that which is not in tune with the inner light.

Meditation organizes your mind and develops your discriminative faculty, often called *buddhi*. Once it is developed, you know right from wrong. It can even be called the tuning fork through which you hear the true direction from your Inner Guide and tune your thoughts, feelings, and actions to it accordingly. As you achieve discrimination, your mind becomes more and more organized and reflects greater ideas coming from your inner realms.

Meditation not only organizes and sublimates the mind but also purifies your emotional nature, cleansing your aura of many glamors and hypnotic urges which make your life one of misery. Meditation releases the mind from such slavery and makes your emotional nature a reservoir of unselfish love and compassion. This transformation starts when, through meditation, the focus of consciousness goes beyond the fourth level of the mental plane and sheds greater light on the emotional nature.

Your mental aura must be in equilibrium as far as the substance of the levels is concerned. When they are in a certain proportion, man is sane and mentally healthy, though not necessarily intelligent. But when the proportion of the quantity of substance in the levels of the mind is distorted or disturbed, you lose your mental balance and common sense.

This happens, for example, when you think on low levels and attract low level atoms to your mental sphere but in the meantime do not add any corresponding quantity of higher atoms on the higher levels or in the higher mind. The same thing happens when you attract too many abstract mind atoms without preparing your lower mind with discipline and purification. In this case you will be unable to handle and translate the increasing voltage of the higher mind. This happens, too, when you have been forced or influenced strongly toward great visions and have developed great aspirations. As a consequence you write, you lecture on great ideas and plans, but in the meantime you have hatred, separativeness, and jealousy in your heart which draw you into a different kind of activity in your actual life. There you again create an imbalance. The results are insanity, imbalance, and distortion on all three of your personality levels. Because you are speaking about idealism and acting against it, thinking about high subjects but planning for destructive actions, you will draw high atoms and low atoms in a proportion that will totally disturb the balance of the mental plane.

The proper way to progress on the mental plane is sublimation. The lower atoms must sublimate into the sphere of the higher mind. The higher mind must vibrate and draw more vibrant and advanced atoms from the planetary and solar Minds.

The balance or the equilibrium of the mental body is very important from the viewpoint of health because once balance is lost, your health degenerates. The mind acts as a prism, especially for average or a little higher quality people, and it sustains the nourishment of the centers.

Mental education does not necessarily help your emotional development. The mental plane develops, unfolds, and blooms not through collecting knowledge or data stored in your mental storehouse but through right meditation.

We have so many informed people in various fields and in various high positions who are full of greed, fear, hatred, jealousy, and vanity, and their minds are totally devoted to serving the ends of greed, fear, hatred, and vanity.

The third plane of the mind is where your Inner Guide operates and the light of your Intuition starts to penetrate into the astral plane. When you are functioning on the lower mental planes (7,6,5,4), you are in conflict with your own life. But when you enter the third plane, you enter into the rhythm and symphony of the Inner Lord.

Kama-manasic consciousness is a consciousness where the lower mind is mixed with the emotions and man is in conflict between his visions, hopes, and expectations and the chaotic life of his personality. At that stage the emotions rule and the mind serves the emotions. The man lives through the command of his emotional drives and urges instead of through the leadership of his reason and logic.

Purification of the astral plane helps the astral centers to unfold and be highly active. Any center that is forced into activity before such a purification leads into lower psychism.

We must state here that there are three principal ways of thinking: thinking within the mental sphere, thinking under the light of the Soul, and thinking through the light of Intuition. The first is used chiefly by fifth ray people

— scientists — who, through intense focus of mental energy and experiment, find the laws of Nature and use them for their own ends, probably penetrating the mind of the planet and learning how to put its laws to use in practical ways.

The second method is involved chiefly with the laws of unfoldment, transformation, and change of Nature. He who thinks along these lines may have acquired the knowledge discovered by the scientists but he does not use it once he finds out that he may misuse the laws of Nature or he may violate or pollute the natural environment in the future. He is a deeper thinker and will never create the poisonous gases, the machines for polluting the air, sea, and earth, nor will he play with radioactivity that creates obscure problems within the brain of man and hinders his future development. The thinker's interest is according to his level of development. The interest of a deeper thinker lies in the laws of the Soul and its development.

The third way of thinking is of a revelatory nature which may be called contemplation. Here great archetypes are first sensed and then seen and absorbed with a tremendous sense of universality and timelessness. Thoughtforms built upon such revelations lead to simplicity and to a natural environment, and a great sense of responsibility dawns in the minds of the meditators in relation to all forms of life — past, present, and future. A revelatory person can create many mechanical devices, but if these devices are not to be used for the unfoldment of the soul, but rather to lead people into the sphere of vanity, waste, and illusion, he elects not to work on them but chooses to obey the laws of Nature. For him when something is not good for the whole, it is good neither for a man, a group, nor a nation.

Meditation is entering into the light, step by step. First the lower mind must be purified; next a bridge must be built between the lower and the higher mind — the sphere of the Inner Guide; then the meditator must pass into the sphere of the intuitional light. The meditator is going to cultivate his concrete mind, putting his questions in the light of his intelligence and trying to think as a man who concentrates on his mathematical or scientific problems endeavoring to solve them and relate them to as many factors as possible.

Thinking gives us power, and eventually the rulers of the world will be those who are able to think clearly. This is what Plato meant when he said that, in the future, the politicians will be philosophers. Thinkers rule the minds of other people, thereby controlling politics, education, philosophy, arts, sciences, religions, and industry. Meditation is the science of thinking clearly, in the light of the divine Plan and in the focus of the Purpose of creation. All that makes life more meaningful is the result of right thinking. Of course, people can misuse any subject with wrong thinking which works against their own good. The minds of such people are slaves to their emotions or to their physical urges and drives.

Art in its manifold fields; scientific discoveries; law; education; philosophical ideas and visions; great religions; revelations; economic, financial, and communication systems are all the result of thinking.

A few hundred years ago a man wanted to demonstrate the result of wrong thinking. He climbed a tree, sat on a branch four feet away from the trunk, faced it, and started to saw off the branch. People came and warned him that he would fall and land on his head, but he continued cutting....

Wrong thinking is an organized activity without a vision for goodness, beauty, and truth. In sawing the branch, the man used his lower mind, but without thinking. Thinking is always slanted toward survival and most of all toward the expression of beauty, truth, and goodness.

Instead of thinking, some people use mantrams, invocations, or chantings to attract energy or enlightenment. This technique is fraught with great danger as the subject eventually loses control of his vehicles and control over the flow of incoming energies, or light. Creative thinking not only invokes and evokes energy but also builds its vehicles and its mechanisms of reception, assimilation, and expression.

Real meditation is a step-by-step purification, construction, conscious communication, conscious assimilation, and creative expression. It is a steady increase in expansion of consciousness in which things are seen in their proper proportion and in their true qualities.

Mantrams, chanting, and repetition of words create congestion and suppression in the nature of man, resulting in imbalance of mind and emotions.

One day a medical doctor called me and said, "Torkom, what is this? My daughter started to meditate and I don't want her to do that. It is crazy to close the eyes and sit for 15 to 20 minutes." I said, "Did you ask her what she is doing?" He replied, "I don't want to know." I said, "If you want to know, come and see me." One hour later he came to my office. I explained to him that meditation is a technique to calm one's nerves and emotions and to quiet one's mind. It enables one to think creatively, to find the cause through the effect and see the effect through the cause, and then to formulate a more constructive relationship and a better life. "Your daughter was smoking, using various drugs, was not paying attention to her school work, and was wasting her energies without discrimination," I told him, and asked if he had noticed any improvement in her life. "To be honest, yes," he replied, "but I don't want her to meditate." "You mean you don't want her to use her mind and think?" I asked. "All that I am teaching is how to improve one's thinking, and your daughter is doing very well. You became a doctor because you used your mind. This means that we can improve our thinking and, after achieving a considerable degree of information in any field, we can start self-mastery through meditation and prepare ourselves for greater service."

The father was happy when he realized that his daughter was doing nothing wrong. The interesting result is that this doctor now meditates every morning and reports that his sense of responsibility, compassion, and clarity of mind have increased considerably.

Meditation changes our outlook, our responses, and our way of mutual relationships. As it causes changes within us, so we bring about changes in world affairs. Real change starts from within and spreads outward. Repeating mantrams or chanting without using your mind exaggerates your difficulties. Through meditation you may find solutions to your problems by seeing the causes and effects of the problems and by penetrating into the nature of the energies and laws of the Universe.

Meditation is constructive thinking according to a plan impressed upon our higher mind at the time of our orientation, silence, dedication, and focus. Often we are impressed with a plan. Our next task is to discover how to organize our life and relationships according to that plan. This plan is known by many different names: vision, inspiration, high-calling, and the like. Meditation not only enables us to have the vision, but also provides the needed energy and technique to carry it to fulfillment. When one's mind functions under the drive of wrong motives, or under negative emotions and blind physical urges, it functions in the wrong way, and we call this wrong thinking. To counteract the effects of wrong thinking, we must use our mind in right thinking as a result of meditation.

For example, if we wish to eliminate smog from our cities we cannot depend on chanting invocations or mantrams but we must resort to creative thinking, free from greed, separation, exploitation, and short vision. This is also true of the pollution in any field of human endeavor. Life must be reconstructed by a higher way of thinking, and meditation is the path to such thinking. Before our mind has become developed and our motives have been purified, the chanting and mantrams bring in

> congestion
> explosions
> inner turbulences
> suppressions
> obsessions
> materialism or attachment to objects

When our motives have been purified and our mind has become highly developed, certain mantrams may be used for specific purposes. Invocations or mantrams which invoke energy, light, love, or guidance for all humanity — as in the Lord's Prayer or the Great Invocation — are useful means to better the conditions of life, especially when the mantrams are included in reflective meditation.

Meditation is an act of holding our mind in the light of the Soul, trying to purify our personality to discover the answers to our questions, and striving to build a path toward higher levels of awareness, thereby eventually achieving enlightenment. True enlightenment starts when our mind functions in the light of the Spiritual Triad or in the light of the higher abstract mind, Intuition, and Spiritual Will.

How do we start real meditation? First, we must sit quietly, spine straight and unsupported and relaxed. Next, we must decide on a sentence, an axiom, an event, a question, an animal, a tree, a lake, an ocean, or an inanimate object such as a table, a chair, a house, and so on.

Then we must concentrate our consciousness in our mental levels as high as possible and focus our consciousness on our chosen subject. We must start thinking about the form of our subject. Suppose it is a tree. What is the form of a tree, the form of this particular tree, and how does it differ from the form of other trees? Next we concentrate on the quality of this tree — the specific quality that differentiates this tree from all others. It is easy to find its quality if we ask, "What does this tree do or what special influence or effect does this tree have that others do not?" The third step is to find the purpose of this tree — from the viewpoint of the tree, of man, or of the Universe. Then we must think about the cause of the tree — how its form, quality, and purpose came into being.

We must try to find deeper and more meaningful answers to our questions. Such meditation is not a form of idleness but an extreme mental labor which brings about expansion of consciousness, aligns the natures of man, and builds higher roads toward spiritual awareness.

Possibly you choose a virtue as your subject, perhaps gratitude. Sometimes it is difficult to find the form of gratitude, but think, for instance, how a grateful person looks. When a grateful person makes a gesture, his eyes and face look different from the eyes and face of an angry person. Here you can find the form of gratitude, even create symbols to explain its form. Such meditation is also a creative labor in which your mind associates, organizes, and produces manifestations of great beauty.

Such meditation leads your consciousness, step-by-step, toward the higher levels of the mental plane where a fusion with the higher spheres takes place. Your thoughts become invocative and provide the answer, an evocation from higher spheres, and the entire field of your consciousness is enlightened and expanded. After you use your mind from these four viewpoints for ten to fifteen minutes, record the things you envisioned as the result of your meditation.

Continue your meditation day after day, year after year, and eventually you will learn the real art of meditation. It will become a technique of illumination, peace, inspiration, healing, success, and beauty, and you will become a thinker. During meditation, greater help will come to you from Those who watch the striving disciples, and at the right time They will meet you and guide you to a greater labor.

After a year or so, you will have acquired a deeper, more organized thirst for knowledge and wisdom and a greater urge to systematize your life and be of more help to others. Right thinking will increase your energies, your magnetism, and your creativity.

While meditating, always proceed with the method of questions and answers. Ask why, how, when, where, and try to find some answers from the depths of your mind. Or you may visualize a group of people asking various questions about your seed thought which you are trying to answer. This will keep your mind alert and will enable you to penetrate deeper into the core of the seed thought of your meditation.

Your seed thought may be any object or verses taken from the Holy Scriptures or philosophical books or any scientific, educational, or political subject.

Take another subject, perhaps the word peace. What is peace? What form does a man, a nation, or humanity take when peace prevails? How does the environment change because of peace? Why? What happens to our physical body as a whole when we have peace within us? How does it affect our mental and emotional responses? What does peace accomplish for humanity or living beings? Is the quality of peace understanding, unity, creativity, protection?

And what about its purpose? Can we say that its purpose is to create right human relations, one humanity, brotherhood, safety, and freedom everywhere for everybody?

Then the cause of peace can be an intense suffering, wisdom, revelation, the Plan of the Hierarchy, the essential unity of everything, the One "from Whom we proceed and to Whom we return." Some people believe that prayer and invocations are meditation. These may be part of it, but the core of true meditation is thinking — going deeper and deeper into your being and finding the answers to your questions; analyzing, solving, and synthesizing; adapting your discoveries to life in general to bring about a greater urge for beauty, goodness, and truth.

The goal of meditation is not only to transform your nature, but also to enable you to pass from your human nature to your divine nature where you can experience the reward of your long and strenuous labor in meditation. Once you have made this breakthrough, you enter into your divine heritage. You discover that a different life exists beyond the level of human life. You feel the presence of your Soul — and even meet Him. This leads you to your Master, Who will be in charge of your spiritual development during your higher meditations.

Through meditation, Soul contact is established. And as the disciple strives to bring the radiation of that contact into his daily life expressions — through intelligent love, service, purity of motive, gratitude, joy, simplicity, courage, and harmlessness — his contact with the Soul gets closer and more frequent. This increases his magnetism and eventually his aura becomes so magnetic that he begins to register the impressions coming from the Hierarchical Plan or even from Christ Himself. He gradually adapts all his life expressions to the divine Plan and functions as a disciple of Great Ones.

As he continues his meditation and extends his contact to the Spiritual Triad, the disciple begins to register glimpses of the divine Purpose. Thus, stage by stage, he initiates himself into greater awareness through continuous and intelligent meditation.

The meditation process is not a wandering in the fields of our present and past memories but an ascension to new territories and summits of enlightenment. Our goal is to explore the treasures of the Unknown. Through our aspiration, spiritual striving, and service, we attract subtle impressions and electric waves of rare knowledge. Often this knowledge is impressed upon the higher planes of our existence, but, due to many reasons, it cannot descend to the physical brain. Meditation, when carried on regularly and consciously, brings these impressions down to brain consciousness. It is at this time that we feel a great upliftment and enrichment. All impressions coming from higher sources are very magnetic and, because of this, meditation raises the magnetism not only of our appearance, but also of our speech, the looks in our eyes, and our written words.

This is why all true servers, who are the initiates in the spiritual spheres, are extremely magnetic and attract to themselves people who need them and who will carry their message further.

This technique of meditating on four viewpoints will be very useful to those who will, in the future, master the Science of Telepathy. Successful telepathic communication cannot be achieved if the message of the symbol is not analyzed through four viewpoints and if the consciousness is not raised and focused upon the higher mental planes. The same is true for the receiver.

Great Ones can communicate with Their disciples when the disciples are aligned physically, emotionally, and mentally and are awake on higher mental planes. The technique of the four viewpoints will be a tremendous help to bring about this effect.

When we are thinking about the form we are exercising the fourth level of our mind. The quality of the seed thought is examined by the third level of the mind. The purpose of the seed thought is examined by the second level of the mental plane, and the cause is examined by the first level of the mental plane. Thus, as we do our meditation, we create integration between these four levels of mind and align them with the Thinker. It is after this achievement that the Great Ones can communicate with the disciple.

This is one of the rounds. In the higher round, when man develops all the layers of the mind and disperses the accumulations of the subconscious mind, the situation will be as follows: The seventh and sixth levels of the mind will be able to see the form, the quality of the form, the purpose, and the cause of the form. In fifth and fourth levels we will be able to see the form of the quality, the purpose, and the cause of the quality. On the third and second levels we will be able to see the form that purpose produces on various levels, the quality of the purpose, and the cause of the purpose. On the first level we will see the form of the cause, the quality and the purpose of the cause, and its true originating source. This will come gradually as we enlighten our minds with the light of the Soul.

Bear in mind that we need levels that deal with the form and quality, and also levels that deal with purpose and cause. The forms and qualities are not only the properties of dense forms but also the properties of subtle forms such as emotional, mental, and even forms built by higher substances. Thus we start investigating the form of an emotion, the quality of a thought, the purpose of a vision, the cause of an urge or intention.

As you know, the mind is divided into two main sections, the lower mind — levels seventh, sixth, and fifth, and the higher mind — levels third, second, and first. The fourth level is a transmitter from the higher to the lower and from the lower to the higher mind. Our intention is to balance the parts of the mind in such a way that there is direct communication, registration, and translation between the two sections of the mind with equal ability.

Without the lower mind we would be lost in space. Without the higher mind we would be totally earthbound. We want to be able to use both sections of our mind in order to have harmonious development and a balanced life. This is why abstract thinking must have the good foundation of the concrete mind, which can be developed by the ordinary sciences given to us in our high schools or colleges or is cultivated in our practical lives of labor and arts and crafts. The main thing is to be able to translate and use the abstract ideas and higher contacts through the lower mind and also find meaning and significance, purpose and cause within the registration of contacts.

It is suggested in one of my books that if we have spent five to ten years in religious, metaphysical, or abstract thinking only, we must take one or two years vacation to study physics, chemistry, biology or work with our muscles as carpenters, builders, electricians, or plumbers so that in the future we are more creative. Creativity is the result of close cooperation between lower and higher minds or between all levels of the mind. The goal of the human soul must be to use all levels at any time.

A highly developed mind has passed through a strange transformation. The atoms of the mind are initiated into a greater light, and eventually the fourth level substance dominates. After a higher initiation, the third dominates, then the second, and then the first level substance of the mind dominates the whole mental sphere. But, with all these changes, man still must have the lower mind highly purified, ready to act as a link between the concrete and abstract levels of the mind, and totally subject to the impressions coming from the higher sources.

At this stage the lower mind does not present any activity of its own. All its contents, which were the cause of its mechanical functions, are cleaned and it stands under the command of the liberated human soul, focused upon the Intuitional Plane.

To create something fundamental and useful, you must have a cause, a purpose, the ways and means or the quality, and the form or the result. This means that for such a creative activity you can reverse the four viewpoints and start to meditate from cause to form instead of from form to cause.

In this case, if you have greater knowledge about the cause, you will have greater success in your purpose, a better quality with which to charge your form, and a better form through which to express the cause. It is very interesting to note that the form is the materialized cause.

Before you start to create or express yourself in any responsible action, you may think about the possible cause of such an action. If the cause is found to be in order with your highest aspiration, then you can investigate the purpose of your creative action.

The purpose is the reason why you want to do the thing that you want to do. This can be a call to meet a need or a responsibility.

Then you go a step down and think about the ways and means with which you are going to express yourself. This gives the quality to your future form.

The next step will be to meditate on the form. The form varies according to your own inclinations and background. It may be a group of people, a picture, music, a dance, an organization, a statue, and so on.

Thus, you can bring a great charge into the form from the cause and make the form adequate to the real cause.

You may also compare the following words:

> cause — the urge, the motive
> purpose — the goal, the direction
> quality — the ways and means
> form — the result, the effect

You can use such a procedure to meditate on any event, starting from the motive to the result or from the cause to the effect.

Meditation thus leads us to a higher level of self-actualization, to the conquest of our lower vehicles, and to a radioactive life in the service of humanity. Those who do not know how to retreat into the inner world and contact higher light and expressions of beauty lean on external supports whenever they meet an obstacle. I know a man who buys a bottle of whiskey and drinks it every time he has a dissension with his wife or children.

He tries to solve his problem with whiskey. This, of course, is an escape mechanism which eventually creates more problems to be handled by such means. Eventually he may lose his reasoning or become a criminal.

Meditation creates freedom; artificial methods of solving our problems create slavery. Some people come to depend on crutches in whatever form they are to be found.[1]

A very beautiful, symbolic event occurred in the life of Christ. One day He and His disciples were crossing a lake in a boat when a great storm came up. The disciples were filled with fear; they wanted to find the Master and ask His advice, but they did not see Him among them. At last they found Him at the bottom of the boat sleeping peacefully.

"Master," they said, "we are sinking! We are in danger!"

He arose, by His willpower calmed the sea, and asked His disciples, "Why were you afraid?"

The boat is the human being in whose depth the Soul exists on different levels. When we are troubled or have problems, we must go deep into our being and contact the Lord through meditation; then the awakened or active Lord will handle our problems and lead us into peace. True help always comes from that Inner Lord. You cannot, either physiologically or psychologically, provide permanent help to a person unless you awaken the Inner Lord within him. Once this Inner Lord awakens, the troubled man will find peace and proceed on his way. This Inner Lord is Willpower, a sleeping tiger. Some

---

[1] See *The Hidden Glory of the Inner Man* by Torkom Saraydarian, Ch. 14.

people, instead of going inside, deep, deep into their being to seek the hidden Master, try to find help through drugs, alcohol, or other artificial, mechanical supports. The only hope for a human being is to contact the inner Master through meditation. There are people who believe they can solve their problems with drugs or alcohol. For example, if a shy person is required to give a speech, he may resort to drugs or drink and thus become talkative; or when a person is unable to make love because of some hang-ups, he may use stimulants. The problems are not being solved but merely suppressed or held in abeyance for a time; they will return later, stronger than ever. There is another disadvantage to using drugs. When a person is under the influence of drugs, he is susceptible to post-hypnotic suggestions which take possession of him, and, in due time, he loses control over his body, emotions, and mind.

After contacting the Inner Guide through meditation and charging ourselves with sufficient energy, we must face our problems and try to find a solution to them. Through meditation we touch the sleeping fire within us which eventually helps us take control of our life and actions.

We are advised not to dwell on our problems but to contact the Inner Guide, raising our level of consciousness up to His level. Once the Inner Lord awakens, we will find that most of our problems have disappeared. A boy once told me that he could not find a job although he had searched diligently. I said, "The problem is not that no job exists but that your mind is troubled. When you remove that trouble, you will find a job."

The Inner Lord must be awakened through meditation and given control over your life. Meditation creates

Soul infusion. Your physical, emotional, and mental bodies are penetrating into the light, and, once you have entered into the light, no problem can depress you or cause you trouble. On the contrary, a problem brings greater challenges and joy because on that level each problem becomes a game and a means to exercise your power and awaken and bring into play your latent abilities. A man who is really Soul-infused uses every mounting wave to achieve better surfing. People who are in contact with their Inner Lord through meditation find that the Inner Lord inspires them with courage, daring, and increasing joy in solving problems. Problems are opportunities for service, sacrifice, and creativity.

The Inner Guide is known by many names in various religions and philosophies: "Krishna Consciousness," "Christ Consciousness," the "Inner Buddha," the "Transpersonal Self," the "Big Brother," the "Watcher Within," the "Fountainhead of Creativity," the "Righteous One," the "Source of Beauty," the "Principle of Freedom," the "Golden Bridge," and so on. These names are very significant, but the most important thing to bear in mind is that there is a Presence within the reach of the meditator Who can guide, inspire, strengthen, heal, and release him and Who can lead him forward on the path of evolution and creative accomplishment. All masterpieces in every field of human endeavor are the result of a close relationship between this Inner Guide and the unfolding human soul. The closer man comes to his Soul, the greater the effect his creative actions will have on progressing humanity. The Soul, through Its creative actions, provides the energies that push the wheel of evolution forward toward greater achievement. The Soul communicates with man through deep meditation, and man registers the waves of the Soul's meditation through his accomplishments.

You feel an urge to progress to perfection when you watch the works of art from the age of Pericles or the works of Michelangelo, Leonardo Da Vinci, or Nicholas Roerich. You feel the urge when you read *The Bhagavad Gita*, *The Upanishads*, the *New Testament*, the Agni Yoga books, or the Tibetan's works or when you witness heroic action in any field of human endeavor. The source of all progressive discoveries, arts, and unfoldments is the storehouse of knowledge and wisdom of the Soul — into which we try to penetrate through our meditation and radiate the contents through our service for humanity.

The fact that man, through meditation or pure thinking, finds the answers to his many questions demonstrates the existence of One Who knows, One Who is willing to help, One Who is within our reach.

Meditation strengthens this relationship, causing unfoldment and greater sensitivity in certain glands and in the nervous system. Thought affects the nervous system and glands and arouses into activity many sleeping cells and neurons. Thus, through meditation, our physical body starts its second phase of evolution or refinement which will provide the unfolding human soul with a better mechanism to register the wisdom radiating from the Inner Guide.

Truly psychic people are those human beings who have surpassed their human level and now are entering into the domain of their divinity, into the heritage of their essential core, unfolding their mechanism a step further, and thus providing a better communication line between the Creative Center and man. This is the reason why such people are highly creative. They see greater visions; they have access to higher planes and can express their spiritual experiences in their creative expressions.

A highly creative artist is a normal psychic who reaches such a degree of development only through meditation and creative service. Meditation not only enables us to attract greater ideas and visions but also enables us to express them through our practical life.

For example, suppose a man is meditating on the seed thought of peace through four viewpoints such as:

What will be or what is the form of life that peace can produce?

What will be the quality of peace?

What will be the purpose of peace?

And what will be the cause of peace?

In a few months' time the person will really attract to his mind all those ideas about peace which will provide for him a new approach to life, and eventually he will think, feel, and act motivated by the spirit of peace.

This is just an example. We may do the same with other seed thoughts and expand our consciousness day after day to such a degree that we begin to tune in to the impressions coming from our Soul and thus find the path to greater wisdom and creativity.

Some people think that chanting is a form of meditation. This is not so. Chanting can be done by anyone, but only those whose minds are educated can meditate. This is why all our mathematical problems, problems of service, politics, and business, or the striving for survival help to cultivate our mind and make us ready for meditation — which is thinking in the light of goodness, beauty, and truth. You cannot solve your car's problem by standing beside it and chanting for one day, nor can you heal a broken leg by chanting; you must use your mind. Meditation is the creative use of your mind for greater enlightenment, goodness, and beauty. Chanting increases your energy at best; it does not offer guidance. It does not discriminate between actions you are going to take. The increase of energy can flood your system, increase your vices, and drive you insane if you do not have sufficient preparation to digest and express the energies constructively. It releases many guarded subconscious urges waiting to escape, and often people fall victim to these rushing floods of suppressed elements from their past lives or from their subconscious minds.

Meditation is a process of formulation and translation of those impressions and inspirations which pour down into the mind at the time of personality and Soul contact.

In our television set an analogous phenomenon is taking place. The vibrations, or the waves of impressions, are coming into the set where they are changed into pictures, sound, and color. The mind has a similar function at the time of meditation.

During chanting, you evoke energy from unknown sources. This puts your mechanism in contact with non-human entities. In this case you do not have control of the incoming energies, the ready equipment to use them, or the means to recognize the source of these incoming energies. This situation creates a real danger for the chanting one, especially when the person is not directly instructed by a Great One and watched by Him.

Meditation creates a direct channel between you and your Soul. Chanting more often builds communication between you and deva kingdoms, whose influence upon the unprepared one is always destructive because man cannot yet hold their vibrations.

Deep meditation is not advised for people who do not have right motives and love in their heart or a purified mental, emotional, and physical nature. Such people must wait until, through discipline, they prepare their lower natures to absorb safely the energies released through meditation.

There are also people who use certain kinds of meditation to arouse the fire at the base of the spine, the kundalini. This can have dire consequences on their physical bodies and on their mental mechanisms. Thought energy must not be directed to any center in the etheric body nor to any gland in the physical body but must be used to explore the Space of thought, the Mind of the Universe. When your consciousness expands and you tune to the Mind of the Cosmos, you unfold without working directly on your centers. Kundalini fire is released naturally in proportion to your expanding consciousness and the purity of your nature, just as in a thermometer the mercury rises as the heat in the atmosphere increases. Those who try to raise the kundalini fire eventually burn either their mental, emotional, or etheric centers, predestining a horrible future for themselves in the coming years or lives. Sometimes the effect does not appear for a long time on the physical plane, but the destruction will persist in subtle levels and make the subject the prisoner of the form which eventually will shatter, causing great suffering.

Only Great Teachers, those who have the power to see and direct energy through their third eye, can teach the disciple how to use the fire of kundalini when it has been released through the purity of his life and through sacrificial service. They may also teach how to purify and cleanse obstacles from our threefold vehicles and how to expand our consciousness in sacrificial service so that the fire is released naturally and provides a sustaining storehouse of energy to be used for the great labor of spiritual liberation.

Meditation creates a magnetic pull on the higher mental plane, and all the lower energies slowly become oriented toward it. This creates sublimation of the lower forces, alignment in the threefold personality, and eventually the lowest center with all its potency begins its ascent. This is how our problems are solved. When we raise our consciousness above our problems and meditate, we become aware of the causes of our miseries and how to overcome them. It is not pity or emotions that solve our problems but a mind that thinks right.

For instance, if your car has a flat tire and you sit down and start pitying it or chanting mantrams or getting mad, you will find that the tire remains flat. But by using your mind, you can find the solution to your problem.

Even love by itself cannot solve our problems if it is not turned into pure reason through meditation. An average man who loves someone without using his mind will have problems sooner or later. If he considers the many factors involved in love, his problems may be reduced.

Meditation is not only the use of the mind in constructive and creative ways, it is also a bridging process between the mental plane and Intuition. It is through this bridge that love becomes pure reason, the heart center in the head unfolds, and the mind is purified of all its illusions and reflects the lights of the higher realms. Such a mind is truly a great revealer and reflector of inner glories.

Once someone asked me whether he should meditate when he is emotionally upset, and he asked how one can become calm if he does not meditate at this time. My answer was, do not meditate unless your mind is calm and clear. Any attempt while you are emotionally upset will cause your mind to become a slave to the emotions and to serve them. You should also be very careful in making a decision when you are upset. It is better to wait until you are calm and normal before making the decision, except in rare cases.

Before you meditate, peace must envelop your mind, emotions, and body. Then you must turn the searchlight of your mind on your seed thought. At this time you are not trying to solve any emotional or physical problem; rather, you are gathering energy and exercising your mental muscles so that they will be able to overcome any problem they may meet later.

It sometimes happens that our consciousness is stuck in the lower levels of the mind and repeats the contents of the lower mind, and we call this meditation. We must know that the lower mind is the storehouse of clichés. When you start raising your focus of consciousness from the lower to the higher mind, new visions, new ideas, new energies are contacted and you feel that you are on a higher level where you are touching inspiring waves of new revelations. During meditation the three lower layers of the mind are in suspension, but not the brain. The unfolding human soul, working through the mind, receives the ideas, impressions, and inspirations coming from the Soul via the causal body and formulates them through the fourth level of the mind according to the need at the time.

The true purpose of meditation is to remove from the unfolding human soul the glamors of the astral vehicle and the illusions of the mental vehicle, and to prepare him to stand in the light of the Soul and channel this light to the threefold personality for the use and service of his fellowmen.

The time will come when, through meditation, the unfolding human soul will not only liberate himself from illusions, glamors, and inertia but will also be able to withdraw himself from the physical, emotional, and mental bodies and contact the Great Ones functioning on the Intuitional Plane. Once this has been achieved, man will have found the true depth of everlasting peace, serenity, light, and joy and have contacted those laws and energies which will uplift humanity and heal its wounds.

Today there is much discussion on the energy crisis. There will be no shortage of energy when man finds the reservoir of all energies, which is pure reason or true love. We have no shortage of anything except love, light, and goodwill. When we have these, there will be no shortage. This reservoir of energy is found only through meditation and through sacrificial service.

To sum up, we can say that the process by which the ray of light travels and reaches its source is divided into seven steps. Take, for instance, a paraffin lamp, light it, and then by slowly turning it on with seven small twists you will find that everything around you is gradually becoming brighter. This is the story of illumination. Long ages ago, man was a dim light in the thick clouds of matter. Gradually, his light increased until it illuminated all relationships: his family, his nation, and the world. Many people try to become a light for others before becoming a light for themselves, but this only leads them into darkness. A lamp that cannot illuminate itself is an extinguished light, no matter how it reflects the lights of the world.

The seven steps of meditation are the steps which man must take to approach the light within, to find himself and to become HIMSELF — a point of light. We can define the steps as follows:

The first step is the state of aspiration when the heart, feeling empty, aspires to a higher state of being.

The second step is the state of concentration. The goal is felt and sensed, and the whole power of heart and mind concentrates upon the path and the means leading to the goal.

The third step is the state of deeper meditation in which the heart and mind commence to assimilate the divine Purpose of life and to purify the inner and outer man in order to build the divine Chalice, the Lotus.

The fourth step is the state of contemplation in which the mind is impressed by the divine Presence and starts to glimpse the divine Plan for humanity as a whole.

The fifth step is the state of illumination in which the light pours down from higher levels, bringing greater knowledge and understanding.

The sixth step is the state of inspiration. Here the divine Will begins to express itself through man, who has become a source of divine power and energy. To this state belong all geniuses in the fields of art, leadership, science, philosophy, psychology, and religion.

The seventh step is the state of identification. Man now becomes one with the Will of God. The Golden Bridge is built and the lover and the Love become one. Man reaches his divine source of Light. "God is Light and there is no darkness in Him." All darkness disappears when man reaches the state of true identification.

This becomes possible only when man continuously detaches his true Self from the three lower planes, and from their glamors and illusions, and becomes one with the glory within him as his true SELF. It is through such steps that he is introduced by his Guide to the Teacher of all humanity, the Bodhisattva, the Christ.

Through meditation, enlightenment, and inspiration he creates those conditions in which the contact will be possible, and his threefold personality will eventually reach such a degree of purification that the contact will not create or stimulate any vanity, glamor, or illusion.

The way to Christ is through steady meditation, purification, and selfless, sacrificial service. Meditation is the process in which the Inner Guide watches the threefold personality, pouring down Light, Love, and Power. The radiation of these three energies into our daily life and environment is called service. Through service, the human soul contacts the inner light, and in that light he sees the greater light — the Christ.[1]

MEDITATION TO CONTACT THE CHRIST

The following meditation is suggested to those who want to prepare themselves to meet Christ when He reappears among men and to those who are willing to be impressed and initiated by Him into greater mysteries, to serve His Plan for humanity, to spread peace, to actualize the Brotherhood of humanity, and to remove misery from the face of the world.

---

[1] Please read *Cosmos in Man*, Ch XI, "Visualizing the Master," by H. (Torkom) Saraydarian, pp. 105-108.

The Meditation[1]

1. OM. OM. OM.
2. Salutations to the Prince of Peace, the Head of the Hierarchy, the Teacher of angels and men.
3. OM.
4. Visualize a triangle of golden light uniting three mountain tops and at the center of the triangle visualize another summit upon which stands a five pointed star radiating white rays. The other points of the triangle are shining as suns.
5. Try to visualize a forest of pine trees near the central mountain and find a path leading to the summit.
6. After a while see a fountain and a lake. Enter into the lake and cleanse your body of all earthly attachments. Then continue your journey.
7. Closer to the summit see a stream of fiery energy, and try to pass through it while visualizing that the liquid fire is penetrating into your emotional nature, filling you with compassion for all living beings.
8. Much closer to the summit sit on a rock and look at the shining point in the light of which Christ stands.
    Think for a moment, is there any activity in your life that stands between you and the Lord? Are there any emotions that cannot stand in His presence? Does any thought blur your eyes when you try to look at His eyes?
    After you find a few obstacles on your path to the Lord, try to decide to get rid of them in any way you

---

[1] Please read *The Science of Meditation* by Torkom Saraydarian for deeper information about the steps.

want. The communication or the interview with the Lord is a matter of frequency and tuning in. When you create the right conditions, conscious contact will be possible.
9. Say the following mantram:

The living Sacrifice of the world.
The living Beauty on our path.
The Resurrection and fiery Fountain of love and life.
I come to Thee with a pure heart
and surrender myself
To You.
For the service of humanity,
For the fulfillment of the Plan,
For the glory of Your reappearance.
I stand in Your Presence —
Charge me with the Spirit of love, of light, and power,
That I may follow Your path of resurrection,
Of sacrifice,
Of love.

10. OM. OM. OM.
11. Meditate for 15 to 20 minutes on one of the following seed thoughts:

   a) The Law of Right Human Relations
   b) The Principle of Goodwill
   c) The Law of Group Endeavor
   d) The Principle of Unanimity at-one-ment
   e) The Law of Spiritual Approach

f) The Principle of Essential Divinity[1]

The Tibetan Master when speaking about the Reappearance of Christ said:

> ... *I used the words: "An united world group given to unanimous and simultaneous meditation . . . for the jurisdiction of the Christ." . . . The task is, through meditation, to establish the knowledge of and the functioning of those laws and principles which will control the coming era, the new civilisation and the future world culture. Until the foundation for the coming "jurisdiction" is at least laid, the Christ cannot reappear; if He came without this due preparation, much time, effort and spiritual energy would be lost. Therefore we must assume . . . that there must be organised — in the near future — a group of men and women in every country, who, under due and proper organisation, will "simultaneously and unanimously" meditate upon those juridical measures and those basic laws upon which the rule of Christ will be founded. . . .*[2]

The same applies for all of us who want to meet Him individually. Certain psychological and spiritual conditions must be provided before conscious contact is established with Him. Meditation upon "The

---

[1] These are called "The Laws and Principles of the Kingdom of God."
[2] Bailey, Alice A., *Discipleship in the New Age*, Vol. II, pp. 236-237.

Laws and Principles of the Kingdom of God" will draw us closer to Him.
12. After your meditation, visualize a fiery stream of love coming out from the center of the star and encircling you, causing a total transfiguration of your being.
13. Bow to Him in fiery respect and adoration and say the Great Invocation.
14. OM. OM. OM.

This will take 15 to 20 minutes. After this meditation you will be very careful of your actions, emotional reactions, speech, and thoughts so that in no way will you disturb the spiritual peace you attained.

Do this meditation once every week for two years, then every day for the remainder of your life in addition to your daily meditation. Use each sentence or seed thought for ten successive meditations, every time trying to go deeper and deeper into the meaning of your seed thoughts.

24

▲ Apostolic Succession ▲

A MAN IS AN APOSTLE if he has contact with Christ — anytime, anywhere — and not necessarily with Christ when He was teaching on the banks of Galilee.

The authority to teach and to officiate at the sacraments cannot be given by any bishop or any church but by the Soul of the individual who proves himself to be a disciple through a life of sacrificial service, beauty, simplicity, and a deep sense of responsibility.

In the modern understanding, one is a true disciple of Christ if he is in contact with his own Soul and, through his Soul, with the Christ. Neither titles, positions, nor grades confer on anyone the state of being a disciple or a minister of Christ. Priesthood or ministry is not based upon knowledge, diplomas, studies, or "authority" but is based upon our inner, conscious communication with our Soul, with Christ, and upon the resultant life of sacrificial service. There are many beautiful individuals who have sacrificed and are sacrificing their lives for the upliftment and for the liberation of humanity. They have one authority — and that authority comes from their being an Initiate.

It is interesting to know that for the first two initiations it is the Christ Who officiates, with the help of two other Masters, and through some very mysterious ways the disciple is accepted into a greater field of consciousness and into a greater field of responsibility and service.

It can be expected that the orthodox Christian will at first reject the theories about the Christ which occultism presents; at the same time, this same orthodox Christian will find it increasingly difficult to induce the intelligent masses of people to accept the impossible Deity and the feeble Christ which historical Christianity has endorsed. A Christ Who is present and living, Who is known to those who follow Him, Who is a strong and able executive and not a sweet and sentimental sufferer, Who has never left us but Who has worked for two thousand years through the medium of His disciples, the inspired men and women of all faiths, all religions and religious persuasions; Who has no use for fanaticism or hysterical devotion but Who loves all men persistently, intelligently and optimistically, Who sees divinity in them all and Who comprehends the techniques of the evolutionary development of the human consciousness . . . these ideas the intelligent public can and will accept.[1]

All true disciples are priests unto the Lord.[2]

---

[1] Bailey, Alice A., *The Externalisation of the Hierarchy*, pp. 589-590.
[2] *Ibid.*, p. 514.

25

▲ THE TEACHING OF CHRIST[1] ▲

IF YOU READ THE TEACHING of Christ very closely, very deeply, you will see that in that Teaching from the beginning to the end Christ is emphasizing freedom. It is not only political freedom, social freedom, and so on but also an essential freedom. That essential freedom is the elimination of all those limitations and obstacles that are preventing the human being from returning to his Divine Nature. Everything that prevents you from being yourself, your essential Self, is an obstacle, is a limitation, and the Teaching of Christ shows exactly how to eliminate these obstacles and hindrances to lead you to total freedom.

Let us take the first freedom. The first freedom is to be the master of your body. If you are not the master of your body, you are not free. You are the slave of your

---

[1]From a lecture given by Torkom Saraydarian, September 12, 1993.

body. Christ's intention was to urge us and make us strive toward mastery of our physical, carnal nature. All blind urges and drives that are coming from our bodies must be controlled, must be sublimated, must be transmuted. Once He said, "Be perfect as my Father in Heaven is perfect."

People did not see behind these words the Teaching for freedom. How can you be perfect if you are the slave of your physical body? How can you be perfect if you are the slave of your negative emotions, hatred, anger, fear, jealousy, revenge, separatism, and these kinds of things? In all departments of human nature, you can see this slavery going on. Christ's intention was to make you perfect.

Perfection is the elimination of all hindrances, of all obstacles that are preventing you from reaching that perfection. Even physical body sickness is nothing else but a slavery, a lack of perfection. If your body is really perfect, you do not have sickness. Perfection is reached when you really dominate and conquer everything in your nature which is imperfect, limiting. How do you feel when you are healthy? You feel very free. If you are sick, you are not free.

Also, we need freedom from our mind. In India they say that the mind is the slayer of the truth, of the facts. The mind manipulates.

The mind is very important, but when it runs in reverse gear and runs the show, then it produces all the misery we have in the world. The mind must be cleaned, and man must be free from his own mind. What is in the mind that we must free ourselves from? There is our superstition, our separatism, our fanaticism, our ego, our vanity, our greed. Unless we emancipate ourselves from these six vices, we will not be free human beings. You can be in a prison and still be the most free man in the world. If you do not eliminate your ignorance you are not free because freedom is the elimination of ignorance. As long as you are ignorant, you are a slave of wrong ideas, wrong thoughtforms, and wrong opinions. And with all these, you work against the laws of Nature because you are ignorant. Every time you work against the laws of Nature, you destroy yourself. Every kind of ignorance is self-destructive.

The concept of freedom can be introduced into the seven fields of human endeavor. For example, in politics the ideas of freedom, real democracy, synthesis, unity, and cooperation must be introduced, and the politician must be highly educated and charged with these ideas. In the political field, since the birth of humanity, we have been striving for freedom without understanding what freedom is. If you are a powerful nation and you can destroy other nations, you are not free because you are acting under your instincts, under your separative interests. Freedom is to make every nation free, every nation cooperative, every nation harmonious. If you do not do that, you will continue to the end, until the last judgement, causing pain and suffering for humanity.

In education the principle of freedom must be expressed as inclusiveness and the recognition of the value in all individuals, groups, and nations — always encouraging diverse viewpoints and approaches.

Education is not free. Education in many, many places, even in the universities in the most advanced nations, is not free. I was reading a scientific book. Two scientists were talking and one said, "We have a formula here but it is not working; the same formula was found in Russia and it was working, but because they were Communists we did not accept their formula." Do you see the slavery of mind? The truth has no place there.

In communication the principle of freedom must be thought of as freedom from superstition, prejudice, bias, self-interest. Such a freedom cannot be achieved by any communicator or reporter if he is not trained how to be selfless, accurate, discriminative, and free from his negative emotions and interests.

There is no freedom in communication, in reporting, in the media. Do you think that the media is free? The media of the world is not free because the people who are reporting are not free people. They have their sides, their interests, their fears. These are limitations. If you are emancipated from your own limitations, you can be a real reporter, you can see things exactly as they are. Then you can put in your reporting the vision of the future perfection, the future beauty of humanity, so that you challenge humanity not to feel day and night the crime, the negative news that is going everywhere, but you give humanity hope, vision, and the striving toward perfection.

In the field of the arts the principle of freedom must be expressed by showing people how to sublimate and transform and transfigure their consciousness, how to evoke their own striving toward harmony, beauty, and perfection. Art should be a victory over every kind of ugliness.

Even art is not free. You turn on the television and you see crime, nothing else. This is because most of the people who are creating these films are themselves criminal, are themselves enslaved in sex, in greed, in hatred, in jealousy, in fear. What can they give to humanity? That is why humanity is not advancing. The primary goal of Christ was to make us free from all such activities which waste human resources and do not lead us to the path of freedom.

In the scientific field the principle of freedom must be used to dispel ignorance, prejudices, limitations to striving. Science must be used to alleviate the pains and sufferings of humanity and to free humanity from the pollution spreading everywhere.

In the religious field the principle of freedom must be taught to set the human soul free to communicate with its Source and to manifest all those qualities which will bring to humanity understanding, cooperation, and compassion.

In the financial or economic field the principle of freedom must be taught to stop exploitation and manipulation and to increase the sharing of the offerings of our planet for the enjoyment of all humanity.

A person once said to me, "Christ said, 'Take your cross and follow after Me.' There is no freedom in these words." I said, "There is the greatest ideal of freedom in those words. When you crucify your etheric, physical, emotional, and mental bodies, you achieve resurrection."

The cross symbolizes the personality with its four elements: physical, etheric, emotional, and mental. Until you as the human spark are crucified on this cross and resurrected, you cannot reach your essential freedom.

A man must realize that he, as a spiritual unit, is crucified. He must seek his emancipation from the cross as Christ did. The greatest victory in this world is not to die on the cross but to resurrect yourself from the cross.

What is crucifixion? It is not what the religious people have said it is. It is to totally dominate and conquer your lower nature. When you conquer that, you are in freedom.

From now on when you read the *New Testament*, think about it and you will realize that everything Christ said was about freedom. He spoke about nothing else except freedom plus harmlessness. Freedom without harmlessness turns into violence, totalitarianism, into crimes, into a superiority complex, into destruction. You must have freedom, but freedom must be exercised through harmlessness. If you do not have harmlessness and you feel free because of your weapons, because of your body, because of your intellect, because of your money, because of your properties, you only think you are a free man. But that freedom manipulates people, exploits people, kills people, destroys people because it is not directed by harmlessness.

Harmlessness is compassion, and compassion is nothing else but love, and love is nothing else but freedom. It is so beautiful. When a girl falls in love, she is so free. Imagine if that girl is falling in love with truth, with great visions and ideas, how free she is going to be! Freedom needs harmlessness.

I was at the seashore one day. I was very tired and went there to relax a little. Two people started playing rock and roll on their radio with the volume up very loud. I asked, "What are you doing?" They said, "We are free people. This is the United States of America." I said, "Of course this is the United States of America. They didn't give that freedom to you to take away the freedom of other people." They said, "We never thought about it." "Well, I do not want your loud music. What about my freedom? Shall I pursue my freedom by killing you, beating you? Stop it. I do not want it."

You are going to have your freedom by respecting the freedom of others and being totally harmless. When you impose your freedom, you destroy the freedom of others. To make them free you are going to emancipate them from their ignorance, from their stupidity. It is so important that you think about this because you have neighbors, you have friends, you have wives, you have children. Do you respect their freedom?

I visited a house where a nineteen year old boy lived. He turned up the television very loud while five people were sitting there. His daddy said three times, "Turn the volume down a little lower." But the boy said, "I have my freedom, daddy!" and he increased the volume. What kind of freedom is that? Do you respect those five people, your guests, and do you not care about them? Yes, there is freedom, but with harmlessness, with consideration that other people are also free because God created them free. The greatest goal and indication of freedom is to reach your pure state of blessing, your pure state of Divine Selfhood, so that you conquer your physical, emotional, mental nature and then make efforts to teach people to break their own limitations.

That is why Christ is sometimes called, "The Redeemer." "I redeemed myself from the hatred that I had. I was hating my neighbor for one hundred fifty years." How long are we going to hate and let that hatred create physical, emotional, mental suffering, pain, expenses, bankruptcy, and so on? Hatred is creating all these things.

Okay. You got rid of the hatred that you had. What about the hatred that other people have? You must redeem them from their own hatred, ignorance, stupidity, jealousy, fear, anger, vanity, ego, separatism.

If you are separative, you are limited. You are not a free person. You think only about yourself. You have a superiority or inferiority complex, and these two complexes are the sources of various diseases in your physical body, in your emotional body, in your mental body. All the diseases in your mental and astral nature are going to come and express themselves through your physical body. You can see this. Free people are healthy people.

There is another point to which you may pay attention. Free people exist. Slaves do not exist. Free people have existence. Slave people do not have existence because they are the bodies. Only your spiritual nature, your soul exists. If you do not have a soul, if you do not become your own spirit, your own Self, you are living as a body. You are fertilizer, nothing else. You come into this life without a goal, without a purpose. You are living at the expense of others. To live at the expense of others is the worst kind of slavery. Unfortunately, we often encourage others to live at our expense.

There was a drug user who came to my Center in Agoura and he said, "Why are you so angry about drug users? I am using drugs. I am not doing anything to you." "Well," I said. "You are committing crimes, you are killing people, you are driving on the freeway and causing big accidents. Who is paying for all these? Because of your stupidity all these good people are paying for you. We are paying for your imprisonment, for your meals in the prison, for your psychiatrist in the prison. Do you see where this leads to? You are making us pay for your stupidity. Please free us from these obligations."

Every time a crime is happening, we are paying for it. How beautiful if we change human nature and bring humanity closer to perfection, better and better! Our taxes will be reduced to a minimum because most of our taxes are paying for crimes. Criminal people are not free people. That is why they are criminal. Every enslaved person is a criminal. Look what happened to Russia as a big nation. Communism was based on slavery. It was based on separatism and hatred, the Iron Curtain, materialism. They bankrupted themselves because slavery is not a principle. Freedom is a principle. We must arrange our lives in a way that slowly, slowly we become free people.

A man came to my lecture and said, "May I ask a question?" I said, "Yes." He got up and gave me a lecture. I asked, "What is your question?" but he continued his lecture. I said, "Sit down. You are a slave of your need to show off and your vanity. You are not a free man."

He said, "I am a free man. I am living here." "But," I said, "you are smoking, daily, one pack of cigarettes. You are a slave of that cigarette. How can you talk about freedom, when you yourself are the prisoner of your urges and drives?"

There is "Friday night" slavery. Millions of people are furious Friday night if their girlfriend, boyfriend, wife, or husband does not take them out. They commit suicide. It is slavery. They are slaves to their customs and habits, and so on. If the wife is gone twenty days, the husband dies because he is the slave of his sex, of his jealousy, of his body.

"My husband was dancing with another woman. I will kill him." Do not be the slave of your jealousy.

Christ gave the Teaching because He wanted to emancipate us from jealousy, vanity, and the body.

Christ said, "You are Gods and the Most High lives within you." This means your depression, your inferiority complex, your stupidity, your hopelessness have no power. You know that if God is within you you can do anything, everything in the world. Christ, through His Teaching, can emancipate you from animalism, from your inferiority complex, from your stupidity, from your hopelessness. He said, "You are Gods. You are not that guilty man. You are not that sinner. You are not that ignorant man. God is within you. You are God." These are challenges to live as Gods.

Imagine a boy who has five or six pictures of animals. He says, "Daddy, do you know what I am? I am that monkey," and he is so happy that he is that monkey. He says, "Mommy, that coyote is me, that lion is me, that serpent is me, that goat is me." If you take that boy and say, "No, you are not those animals. You are a beautiful human being," you can emancipate him. You can even redeem him from his animal nature by telling him, "You are not those. You are a Child of God."

I tell people, for example, "You are not your hatred." A lady came to me and said, "My greatest wish is to kill my husband." I said, "What kind of slavery is that? Why are you living in that thought, in that intention? Can you free yourself from that thoughtform or ugly emotion?"

Try to free people. There is no greater help than to set people free. There is no higher joy than to see people free.

All Great Ones are here to set us free. If one of you wants to write a book in the future, write about that all great Ones spoke about one thing: to make us free. Buddha said, "All of you have the Buddha nature within you." Buddha nature is that Almighty, Universal Spirit, all Light, all Wisdom, all Love, all Beauty. That is what freedom is.

Christ said, "Do not worry about what you are going to eat tomorrow. See the birds. My Father takes care of them."

People said that we cannot build a new Temple here in Sedona. If you are Gods, if you have faith that God will provide everything for you, it is impossible that you will not be successful. That is freedom.

"Do not worry about tomorrow. . . ." This is freedom from your worries, from your anxieties.

I ask people, "Why are you worrying? Why do you have headaches?" They say, "I am worrying about what kind of death is waiting for me or when I will get sick." Think of something beautiful. Do not worry about it. God will take care of it. Bless your life with the power of optimism, joy, and daring. Do not invite failure, pain, and suffering through your pessimism.

One of the greatest freedoms is freedom from your karma. How much do you owe to people? How much do you owe for those smiles, that friendship, for those letters and cards, for the help that is given to you, for nice telephone calls, for the encouragement that people gave to you? How much do you owe? These are on the list of your karma, on your bill, plus all crimes that you committed — physical crimes, emotional crimes, mental crimes. As long as you are the slave of your karma, you do not have freedom, but you can overcome your karma by striving toward perfection. Every step toward perfection erases millions of tons of karma from your life, so strive toward perfection.

Another freedom is forgiveness. Did you know that forgiveness is freedom? As long as you cannot forgive, you are a slave. The greatest emphasis that Christ put in His Teaching was on forgiveness. A man came and asked, "If I forgive my friend seven times, is it enough?" because he was waiting to see if seven times was enough so that on the eighth time he could go and kill his friend. But Christ said, "Seventy times seven is not enough." He meant to forgive and forget because in forgiveness you are not building karma; you are evading karma by not involving yourself anymore with karma.

Sometimes when you have fights and misunderstandings with your beloved ones, friends, and so on, use forgiveness even if you are not going to involve yourself any more in their lives. Forgive because non-forgiveness creates a big octopus-like thoughtform within your mind which sucks your emotional, mental, and etheric body and wipes out your energy. Forgiveness is a road toward health and happiness. You become happier if you forgive. If you do not forgive, your energy leaks. One of the greatest Teachings of Christ was to "Forgive people and get free."

Freedom has fourteen major companion virtues.

1. *Gratitude is freedom from your vanity and ego.* When you understand, when you acknowledge that you are so grateful for many things, you are really freeing yourself from your ego, from your separatism, from your vanity. It is so beautiful to be grateful. M.M. says, "Great is the healing power of gratitude." I saved many, many hundreds of families by teaching them to be grateful to each other. Gratitude works miracles.

A lady came one day and said, "We did all that was possible with my husband, but our problem was not solved."

It is good to try, do not misunderstand me, but the problem was not solved. I said, "Lady, the problem cannot be solved because you are not grateful for that man."

She asked, "Why should I be grateful?"

I said, "That man worked twenty-five years and supported you and you never worked. This is one reason. He raised two children, paid for them. Why is he no good? Did you say to him once that 'I am so grateful. You are so beautiful and I appreciate you'?"

She said, "I do not want to say it."

"Well, you cannot solve your problem through psychiatry and psychology. You are going to solve the problem within yourself and be grateful first of all."

Surprisingly, she tried her best to appreciate him and feel gratitude toward him. She went home, and when her husband came home she opened her mouth to ask why he was late but immediately closed her mouth and said, "You look so handsome." The man's question was this. "Why have you started to see my beauty instead of my ugliness?" because every day that woman had been opening her mouth and criticizing that man or the man had been criticizing the woman.

You cannot reach the freedom of joy, of harmony, of cooperation in your home until you stop criticizing, until you stop beating each other. "You are nonsense, you are this, you are that. I have never seen a man more stupid than you." That man is really going to be stupid and do stupid things. At that time of tension, everything you are saying is going as a post-hypnotic suggestion into his mind. That is why every time you are angry and you say something to your wife or husband, your partner actually becomes that which you hate.

2. *The second virtue that goes with freedom is forgiveness.* Forgiveness takes you out of your prison of self-righteousness. "You are something and other people are nothing." Really?

One day I came to the Teacher and I said, "That boy is not good." He said, "I am glad for your report, but sit down and write down whatever you did this week that was not good."

At first I did not want to write. Then I prepared the list, and it was so big.

Then my Teacher asked, "Now do you have complaints about that boy?" "No!" I said. "I do not." He said, "Come here, come here. Do not escape. Why do you not have any more complaints?" "It is because I saw myself!"

When you see yourself, you free yourself from judging others. One of the principles of Christ was to meet, to face yourself. By facing ourselves we discover the path of freedom.

Read the Teaching of Christ and you will see that He is speaking of freedom and nothing else. Unfortunately, this is not taught to us by any church.

Christ said, "You are Gods." What are the psychological implications, physical, emotional, and mental implications, social implications of such an announcement? If I am God, you are God. How does God exploit the other Gods? How does God hate the other Gods? How can I impose my own ideas on you when you are God? That is where the freedom comes from. Nothing must be imposed if you are a free person. This is the foundation of democracy.

If you are not free but you know the Teaching, you know only the skeleton of the Teaching, not the spirit of the Teaching. When you impose it, you impose the skeleton instead of the spirit of the Teaching. Let them read or not. Let them educate themselves or not. You do your best to awaken them, but if they are not awakened you cannot force them to awaken their consciousness. Let them find it, discover it with pain and suffering or education.

3. *The third composite part of freedom is inclusiveness.* Inclusiveness eventually destroys the thoughtform of separatism that was built millions of years ago in our consciousness. For millions of years people have been taught to be separative. "You are this; they are that. We have this religion; they have that religion. We are sitting here in this part of the world; they are sitting in that part of the world. We are this color; they are that color." It is all separatism. It has entered into our bones and we have become a humanity that bases all its life on separatism. "This is my home; that is your home." It is separatism.

This separatism can really be conquered if you become inclusive. First start with your wife, with your husband. Share all the pains and sufferings and joys of your husband or your wife. If you do this, you are becoming inclusive.

Then you can share all the pains and sufferings and joys of your children. Then you can share the group pains and sufferings.

But we are not free enough to have group consciousness. We think about ourselves. To think about ourselves and forget to be free members in a free group means that some thoughtform, some emotion is controlling us and preventing us from being one with the group. We are the slave of our personality and of its limitations. We do not yet have group consciousness. We do not yet have national consciousness. Look at how many separative groups are working in any nation, devastating the nations.

We say nations, but nations are not a unit yet, a cooperative, harmonized group. Freedom will be to create harmonization because that harmonization will free them from the slavery of separatism. Create national unity. Create international unity. How beautiful it is when we hear that some nations are coming together and creating peace. What about if all nations do this on the basis of righteousness and cooperation!

4. *Fearlessness is a freedom.* As long as you are in fear, you are not free. Fear is the worst kind of slavery and sometimes because of your karma you are in fear, because of your past deeds you are in fear, because of your plans for the future that are criminal you are in fear. You are slaves. You are going to free yourself from your own fears.

A young man came to me and said, "I have one fear."

"What is it?" I asked.

He said, "I fear that one day I will die."

Day and night that fear was eating him. I said, "Instead of worrying about dying, think about how to get your university degree, college degree, or to become a human being, a president, a leader, a teacher."

"No," he said, "this fear is killing me, and this fear is telling me that I do not want to be anything because the end of everything is a coffin six feet below the ground."

I spoke to him about the infinity of the human soul, about the everlasting progress and striving of the human being. Then eventually I gave him *Other Worlds*.[1] It released him from the fear of death. By focusing yourself on the future, you can destroy your fears.

There was a man whose son was eaten by a lion. One day he saw a lion standing between the bushes. He said, "I will get closer. I will kill that lion!" He aimed the arrow, shot it, and then ran toward the lion. Then he saw that the lion was made of stone but the arrow had entered one foot into the stone. How had the arrow penetrated? Later he shot three or four more arrows and saw that they were not penetrating. In a fearless and courageous moment, your energy is tenfold greater. You can do many seemingly impossible things.

One day some people were after us. We were four boys. Their intention was to kill and rob us. We jumped across a precipice which was perhaps seven feet wide. We saved our lives. When we came back, we could not believe how we jumped that precipice! It was fearlessness that did it. Fearlessness brings courage. In your life, in your business, in your studies, in your family life, do not give up. If you give up, you are not fearless. Start a new job. Go to the university. Be fearless because your Father in Heaven is going to take care of you. These are the real words of Christ.

5. *Cooperation is freedom.* Cooperation takes your self-centeredness away from you. The worst limitation is to be centered within yourself. "You know better. You can do better. You have better things. You have the best. You are the best." When you are self-centered, you do

---

[1] *Other Worlds* by Torkom Saraydarian.

not cooperate with other people. Because you do not cooperate with other people, you remain a prisoner within your own ego.

Watch people when they are not cooperating. They are self-centered, like the oyster which is attached to its shell. They are shell attached people. Make them free. Teach them the sense of freedom. Let them go like birds anywhere they want in the spirit of cooperation.

6. *Generosity* is freedom from greed and attachment.

7. *Beauty* is freedom from ugliness and chaos.

8. *Purity* is freedom from all hindrances existing within your nature.

9. *Solemnity* is freedom from lightmindedness, hilarity, and irresponsible expressions.

10. *Love* is freedom from jealousy, limitations, and self-interest.

11. *Joy* is the freedom of the soul from attachment to karmic liabilities.

12. *Service* is the freedom to express all that is beautiful and useful within your being.

13. *Righteousness* is freedom from karma. In righteousness either you do not increase karma or you do not create it. Righteousness also erases your past karma.

14. *Goodwill* is freedom. Man is entangled in illwill, negativity, self-interest, rejection, and in every kind of separatism.*Goodwill is a powerful force which releases us from the interests of the elementals of our bodies, from glamors and illusions, and sets us free to pour out the good that is within our Core.

Question: If in a moment of tension someone says something ugly to you and you forgive him, does that

prevent the post-hypnotic suggestion from entering into your subconsciousness?
Answer: Yes, because in forgiveness you are conscious. In a non-forgiving state, you are unconscious. Every time you are unforgiving, your subconscious mind is wide open. Read *The Subconscious Mind and The Chalice*.[1]

Yesterday a man came from Texas who is a healer. He said, "I am going to get *The Subconscious Mind and The Chalice*." I said, "Good! Buy it and read it."

Most troubles originate from your subconscious mind. This means that as long as you are under the control of your subconscious mind, you are not free people. Whenever Christ spoke against limitations, against obstacles, He was referring to the subconscious mind. He said, "You have so many spirits within you that I must clean you." What were the spirits? In that time and in that place, spirits were post-hypnotic suggestions accompanied by evil entities.

Question: What is the difference between forgiveness and avoiding confrontation?
Answer: Avoiding confrontation is a fear-filled action. You are not fearless; you are afraid. You go into your shell and pretend that you are a very strong and noble man, but at the same time you are avoiding confrontation because you are fearful. You think about your skin more than the truth. If you see that a man is violating the principles of a nation and the population is in danger, not to confront him is a hideous crime. Brave people give their life for principles. Christ did it. I bet they told Him that if

---

[1] *The Subconscious Mind and The Chalice* by Torkom Saraydarian.

He denied all the Teaching that He gave, He would be a King. He said, "Go behind Me, Satan!"

Question: What do you think about free speech?

Answer: It is great if it is based on facts, if it is harmless, if it has no secret motives and does not work for selfish interests nor feed separatism.

Speech is like a fire which destroys its source if the source is unclean. Free speech has seven qualities.

1. It has beauty.
2. It is righteous.
3. It is full of compassion.
4. Its motive is to create joy and the spirit to serve.
5. It tries to free people.
6. It tries to make people strive to the future.
7. It inspires people to be enlightened.

If your speech does not have these qualities, it is not free.

Question: You said that when people have *existence* they have become their own spirit, their own soul.

Answer: First of all you must understand who *exists*. Something that is not real cannot exist. Your body is not real. It cannot exist as a body. Fifty years later that body is gone. Your emotions are not real because they are a body. Mind is body. Who is the one who is *existing*? It is your spirit, your true Self. When you are your true Self, you exist. Then you are free. Your true Self exists because you have conquered all those things which are not the Self. You conquered the not-self. This is a hard pill, but you can swallow it.

Question: When you are a parent and you say something in anger to a child, it is not good, but what can you do to help the child?

Answer: You must take the issue up with him and tell him, "You made me angry and I was wrong, but now you must learn how not to make me angry." Then he will think twice.

If I am climbing on the piano and jumping and dancing there and making my mommy really angry, she should say, "I will not be angry if you do not do that." It is confrontation, but really facing the issue. If you are angry and beat him, he will do more ugly things. You are going to enlighten him. Enlightenment is freedom. There is a Buddhist book which says, "Buddha is the most free person in the Universe because He is illuminated."

Deal with your children in such a way that they learn the royal science of freedom. Teach them how to be free from attachments, from negative emotions, and thoughts. Do not inhibit them. Dissolve their fears. Create conditions in the home, in nations, in humanity so that your children can live in freedom, think in freedom. This is what the Teaching of Christ was and *IS*.

INDEX

permanent 79
physical, tiny life in the 21
attachments 209
Augustus, Emperor 43
aura 232
   mental, equilibrium in 221
authority 256

A

achievements
   recapitulating former 100
Adam 87
Age, Aquarian 124
   Christ's Teachings for 113
Age, New; vision of 126
alcohol 239
Almighty One, Will of the 17
Ancient of Days 12
anger 277
Angel, Guardian
   and Fourth Initiation 106
Anna 33, 35
Antahkarana 176
Apollonius 158
   a letter by 159
   of Tyana 154, 155
Appearances, Cyclic 29
Aquarius, age of; def. 125
Archetypal Man,
see Man, Archetypal
archetypes 224
Armenia, school in 65
artist(s) 25
   def. 242
arts
   principle of freedom in 260
   source of 241
aspiration 23, 233, 248
   upliftment 19
   veil of 172
atom(s) 21

B

baby, coming 61
balance, mental
   a cause of losing 221
Balthazar 51, 52
baptism 66, 101
base of the spine, fire at 244
battlefield, sounds on the 180
beauty 56
   def. 274
Bees Bazen 52
being(s)
   advanced, echoes of 16
   human 198
Bethlehem, meaning of 45
birth
   child taking 49
   of Jesus 46
   of the light within heart 101
blessings 26
blueprint, def. 12
Bodhisattva 249
body(ies)
   etheric, rela. to centers 218
   lives of, and initiation 145
   mental
      emotional, and etheric 61
      equilibrium of 222
   of Masters 146
   physical, energy system of
      rela. to etheric centers 218
bomb(s), atomic 178, 180
brain, meditation and 246
breakthrough 232

breathing exercises 176
bridge(s) 245
   and communication lines 21
   of communication 217
bridging process 245
B(b)rotherhood 67, 126
   of one humanity 125
   World 198
Buddha
   and Christ 84, 182
      rela. to love 84
   attaining Enlightenment 103
   birth of 52
buddhi, def. 221

C

Caiaphas 94
Caspar 51, 52
causal body 246
cause
   materialized; form is the 236
   in meditation 231
   thinking about 236
C(c)enter(s)
   ajna 104
   astral 223
   creative 241
   emotional 218
   etheric, listed 218
   formation of 68
   head, of planet 148, 201
   heart, at Fourth Initiation 105
   in Asia and Greece 64
   in Palestine 65
   man becoming a 24
   of
      education 18
      foot 129
      Great Lives 22
      learning 67
      Love 13
      worship 18
   rela. to etheric body 218

thought energy and 244
ceremonials and rituals, def. 18
Chaldea and Persia 66
Chalice 248
   at Third Initiation 104
   seeds in the 146
change
   def. 149
   real 227
chanting 176, 226, 227, 228, 242, 243
   and mantrams, effects of 228
   mantrams 245
chemistry, inner 62
child(ren) 56, 59, 277
   bringing into the world 57
   coming 55
   in the womb 60
   raising 57
   right atmosphere for 60
   taking birth 49
Chohans, effect of on planet 109
Christ, (The) 24, 33, 83, 86 181, 198, 203, 249
   after the resurrection 64
   and
      Buddha, rela. to love 84
      glamors 209, 212
      I(i)nitiation(s)
         first two 104, 256
         of Enlightenment 84
         Sixth 151
         and Seventh 137
         Third of humanity 84
      Love-Wisdom 84
   as
      bread of Life 45
      goal for humanity 198
      tree 49
   became
      a bridge 12, 24
   Buddha and 84, 182
   call of, response to 217
   Consciousness, def. 87
   contact with 255
   Contemporary Work of 181

▲ INDEX ▲ 281

Cosmic, def. 85
def. 198
did not fail 118
disciple of, def. 255
first One to achieve Mastership 22
following after the steps of 9
historical 85
impressions coming from 217
initiation, second, of 84
inner 212
  basically refers to 85
  Soul in man is the 212
is the Son of man 105
Meditation to Contact 249
names for 84, 93, 125, 251, 263
re:
  Law of Cause and Effect 145
  Law of Reincarnation 145
R(r)eappearance of 252
  Masters working for 207
  work He will do at 207
rela. to
  Buddha 84, 182
  Hierarchy 23
  humanity 190, 198
  Jesus 93, 94, 152, 157
  Judas 162
  Shamballa 201
return of 193
story of 238
Teaching of 257
  for Aquarian Age 113
  in Palestine 113
  purpose of 118
technique(s)
  of to reach humanity 91
  to contact 217
  Today 197
  W(w)ay to 217
    def. 249
  within 128
word Christ, meaning of 84
Christians 9
Christmas tree(s) 49

and gifts 50
cloud of knowable things 25
comets 180
Commandments, Ten 103
communication
  telepathic 233
  with our Soul 255
communion
  with Almighty Presence 12
compass 12
compassion, def. 262
concentration 58, 248
  teaching of 58
conception 56
conflict 223
confrontation 275
Confucius 22
  birth of 52
conquest
  of our lower vehicles 237
conscience 128
consciousness
  being stuck in mind 246
  continuity of 175
    web rela. to 175
  energy rela. to 219
  expansion of 217
  Kama-manasic, def. 223
  rela. to energies 218
  three higher states of 169
contemplation 224, 248
  def. 58
continuity of consciousness,
see consciousness, continuity of
cooperation 273
countries 198
creation 11, 12
  as an organism 11
creative center,
see center, creative
creative thinking,
see thinking, creative
creativity, def. 235
Creator 12
  The, Purpose of 12
crime 265

criminal 238
crises of humanity 121
cross, symbol of 261
crown, symbol of 80
C(c)rucifixion
 Christ and Jesus during 152
 def. 261
crystallizations
 Jesus and battle against 95
culture, rela. to great labor 21
Custodians of the Will 148

D

Dance, Sacred 130
dark forces, see forces, dark
darkness, when disappears 248
death 74
decision 246
delinquency, problems with 60
destruction
 saving humanity from 114
detachment 249
deva kingdoms 243
development, future 224
devices, mechanical 224
disciple(s) 21, 141, 179
 influence of 119
 twelve symbolized 164
 washing the feet of the 124
discrimination 221
discriminative faculty,
see faculty, discriminative
diseases 264
distortion 222
 veil of 171
Door of Initiation 74
dramas 18
drugs 176, 239
Dweller on the Threshold 79, 170, 209
 def. 79

E

economic situation,
see situation, economic
education
 centers of 18
 mental 223
 principle of freedom in 259
Egypt 63, 64
 center in 65
 Jesus in 72
electricity 180
emotions, negative 209
endeavor, human
 fields of, freedom in 259
enemies to new Teaching 30
energy(ies)
 consciousness rela. to 218
 crisis 247
 higher
  best way to channel 177
 rela. to
  consciousness 219
  subtle vehicles 61
  vehicles 62
 sexual
  first initiation and 101
E(e)nlightenment 102, 226, 229, 249
equilibrium of mental body 222
Essenes 65, 66
 Teaching of 67
E(e)ther(s)
 Cosmic 174
 lower
  four 174
  fourth 175
 rela. to veils 177
etheric centers,
see centers, etheric
etheric web, see web, etheric
E(e)volution 21, 22, 241
 conscious, path of 99
 H(h)igher
  paths of 79
  Seven Paths of 108, 109

of
   a nation, how to further 62
   human unit 21
   man 149
   wheel of 240
explosions 176
existence 264, 276
eye, third 244

F

faculty, discriminative 221
fanatics, religious 9
father 55
fearlessness 272
feet
   symbol of 127
   washing of 129
Festivals, three Major 212
fiery sphere, see sphere, fiery
fire
   at base of spine, 107, 244
   of spiritual man, result of 174
   of the Will 20
foot, center beneath sole of 129
forces
   astral, in-rush of 179
   dark 119
   lower 218
   of Shamballa 189
   rela. to subtle vehicles 61
forgiveness 268, 270, 275
form
   in meditation 231
   is the materialized cause 236
   thinking about 229, 237
frankincense 52
free people, see people, free
freedom
   companion virtues of 268
   def. 257
   from
      our mind 258
      your karma 267

      your vanity and ego 268
   ideas of in politics 259
   principle of in
      communication 260
      education 259
      finances/economy 261
      politics 259
      religious field 261
      scientific field 261
      the arts 260
   rela. to harmlessness 262
Freud 211
friction 23
fusion 219
future 11, 25
future development,
see development, future

G

Galilee, meaning of word 45
Gandhi 115
gases, poisonous 224
generosity, def. 274
geniuses 248
Gethsemane 137
   Garden of 162
gifts 49
   at the foot of the tree 50
glamor(s) 209, 211, 221
   analysis of 211
   Christ and 209, 212
   def. 209
   does not stay in our aura 210
   global 212
   how
      formed 210
      grows 210
      to control 211
   of sex 210
   repelling 210
   suppression of 211
   when created 209
glands, effects of thought on 241

goal
  -fitting life, def. 98
  of human soul 236
  of meditation 218, 232
  our, def. 233
Gobi Desert 201
God
  Sons of 16
  Will of 248
  good for the whole 224
goodwill, def. 274
gratitude 11
  def. 268
Great Invocation, The 187
Great Ones, see Ones, Great
Greece, center in 66
group(s)
  consciousness 102, 271
  esoteric 173
  labor 102
  life, mystery of 22
  thinking in terms of 102
Guide, Inner 217, 223, 249
  known by many names 240

H

Hall of
  Blinded Men 172
  Choice 171
    rela. to Initiation 171
    rela. to plane 174
  Concentration 170, 173
  Direction, rela. to plane 174
  Ignorance, rela. to plane 173
  Learning, rela. to plane 173
  Monadic Light
    rela. to plane 174
  Wisdom, rela. to plane 173
halls
  seven 173
  three 169
hang-ups 209
harmlessness 101

def. 262
health 55, 222
  equilibrium rela. to 222
heart center 57, 101
help 238
Hercules 22
heritage, divine 232
Hermes 22, 43
Herod 63
heroes 56
Hierarchy, (The) 18, 19, 22, 51
  each member of the
    achievement of 19
  established seven centers 26
  externalization of 119
  Founding of 16
  Head of 86
    def. 104
  Leader of 84
  members of 16
    and labor 19
    and Their disciples, def. 21
  Plan of 149
  rela. to labor 19
  Teaching of 32
  history of humanity 147
Holy Communion 67
  def. 127
  mystery of 123
Home 12
hope, def. 12
human being, see being, human
humanity 16, 25, 198
  and destruction 114
  brotherhood of one 125
  Christ as goal for 198
  crises of 121
  dangers for 114
  has many global glamors 212
  history and future of 147
  progress of 57
  veils and 212
  vision and plan for 198
    Christ, the model of 198
hypnotic urges,
  see urges, hypnotic

I

idea
  a great 61
  incarnating 59
idealism 222
identification 248
ignorance 259
illnesses 176
illumination 247, 248
illusion 209
image 210
imagination 210
imbalance 222
impressions 233, 236
  coming from Christ 217
  subtle 233
impulsion, veil of 170
incarnation 59
inclusiveness 271
individualizing 22
Initiate
  Fifth Degree 157
  Fourth Degree, lesson for 147
  high degree, and humanity 90
  Seventh Degree, Christ as 157
I(i)nitiation 74, 80, 97, 100
  ceremony, def. 97
  def. 97, 99, 143
  divided into three sections 99
  Door of 74
  effect of on rent 172
  Fifth 106
    five revelations in 107
    first 100
      and economy 101
      and sexual energy 101
      the greatest effort 100
      two, and Christ 104, 256
    Fourth 105, 145, 171
      and
        Causal Body 146
        Guardian Angel 106
        Lotus 145
      bodies of Masters after 146

def. 106
heart center at 105
of Jesus 152
mysteries of 208
of Enlightenment,
  Christ and 84
  Joshua, and 77
of Jesus and Christ 152
path of
  achievement on 97
  def. 98
  when begins 99
  process, def. 100
  rela. to transmutation 145
second 101
  of Christ 84
Seventh 110
Sixth 108, 140
  and Seventh, Christ and 137
  Christ and 151
Third 79, 102, 144
  and the Chalice 104
  def. 104
  of humanity, Christ and 84
  of Jesus 143, 144
insanity 222
inspiration 248, 249
Intuition 223
invocations 226, 228, 231
Ishtar 36
Isis 36

J

Jericho, fall of 77
Jesus 22, 31, 32, 34, 45, 63, 64, 74, 89, 90
  after crucifixion 154
  and
    Apollonius 141
    Christ 157
      rela. to Initiations 143
    Inner Temple 150
    Essene Brotherhood 68

Fourth Initiation 145
crystallizations 95
baptism of at river Jordan 90
birth of 46
crucifixion of 149
Fourth Initiation of 152
going to Chaldea 71
in
  Egypt 72
  Greece 71
  Himalayas 70
  India 69
  Persia 70
  school of Buddhism 69
intention of 149
is a man 75
of Nazareth, descent of 74
past lives of 75
rela. to Christ 93, 143, 152
studied and mastered 69
the Christ; becoming 93
Third Initiation of 143, 144
training of
  His immediate disciples 142
visited one of the Magi 70
was a man 75
when beginning to teach 67
Joachim 33, 34
job, finding a 239
John, Peter, and James 142
John at the cross 152
Joseph 41, 42, 51, 52
  of Arimathea 152
Joshua 76
  and Enlightenment 77
joy, def. 274
Judas
  Christ and 162
  purpose of presence of 162
  The Iscariot 161

K

Kama-manasic consciousness
  def. 223

karma 220
Kingdom of God,
  Laws and Principles of 253
Kings 49
knowing yourself 211
knowledge 223
Krishna 52, 84
kundalini fire 102
  release of 244

L

labor(s) 19, 20, 21, 127
  culture rela. to great 21
  Hierarchy rela. to 19
  members of Hierarchy and 19
  organized 21
    Hierarchy, rela. to 19
  sacrificial 19
Law(s)
  of Cause and Effect 145
  of Kingdom of God 253
  of rebirth 208
  of Reincarnation 145
Lemuria 73
L(l)ife (Lives) 172
  Great 75
    centers of 22
  light, birth of 101
Logos, Planetary 15, 147
Lord
  Inner 238
    def. 238
  of the World 81
    The, presence of 129
Lotus 146, 171
  def. 146
  Fourth Initiation and 145
L(l)ove
  Center of 13
  def. 12, 262, 274

M

Magi 52
  The Three 51
  three 50
magic, def. 69
Magnet
  divine 24
  drawing Sparks back 12
magnetism 232
M(m)an
  Archetypal 87
  spiritual, result of fire of 174
  transformation of 18
mantrams 226, 227, 228
  chanting 245
  chanting and; effects of 228
Mary 33, 35, 36, 37, 39, 40, 42, 43, 49, 51, 56, 57
Masonic tradition 74
Master(s) 146, 149
  and leaving of bodies 91
  creating illusory body 91
  Jesus 165
  Koot Hoomi 207
  of Wisdom 107
  using the disciple's vehicle 91
masterpieces 240
mastership of Christ 22
matter and spirit 85
maya 209
media 260
meditation 56, 58, 217, 232, 233, 239, 247, 249
  and transformation 218
  cause, purpose, quality, form in 237
  deeper 248
  def. 217, 220, 225, 226, 227, 229, 243, 245, 249
  effect of on
    lower forces 219
    man 220
    mind and brain 246
  from cause to form 236
  mind in, [conditions for] 246
  on event 237
  on four viewpoints 233
  process, def. 233
  purpose of 246
  questions
    about cause in 231
    about form in 231
    and answers in 231
  real, how to start 229
  rela. to self-actualization 237
  result(s) of 220, 221, 227, 238, 239, 242, 243, 245
  seven steps of 248
  Soul and 240
  strengthens 241
  technique of occult 217
  thinking of form in 229
  to Contact The Christ 249
  true, core of, def. 231
meditator, Presence and 240
Melchior 51
mental aura, see aura, mental
mental balance,
see balance, mental
mental body, see body, mental
mental education,
see education, mental
message of Great Ones 29
mind 245
  atoms of 236
  effect of meditation on 246
  higher 222, 235
  highly developed 236
  is fiery in nature 220
  levels of 234
  lower 235, 236
    def. 246
  subconscious 275
  third plane of 223
  two main sections in 235
  unorganized 220
ministry 255
missions 70
Moses 103, 171
Mother of the World 36

mother(s) 55, 56, 57
  of Mary 33
  real 210
motherhood 57
motive(s) 127, 244
  def. 127
Mount
  Ararat 65
  Carmel 53, 65
music, loud 176
myrrh 52
mystery(ies) 18, 23, 26
  behind Universe 18
  Cyclic Revelation of 17
  def. 23
  effect of on consciousness 19
  Egyptian 64
  intention of 27
  of
    group life 22
    initiation 208
    the Holy Communion 123
  rela. to visions 18
  schools 18, 19

N

nation(s) 272
  schools rela. to change of 62
N(n)ature
  as a great Mother 11
  higher and lower
    fusion between 219
Nazareth 45
nervous system,
see system, nervous
neutrality as a technique 102
New Age, see Age, New
Nicodemus 152
noise 221
North Star 12

O

observation, self 211
obstacle(s) 237, 257
  on the path 79, 209
oneness 128
Ones
  Great 12, 16, 18, 26, 29
    communication of
      with disciples 233
    Message of 29
  Wise 49
Oneself, science of becoming 18
opinion, public 126
opportunity 23
Orion 49
overshadowing 91

P

Palestine, center in 65
parents 59
P(p)ast
  In the 73
  man is result of his 74
path(s)
  most important
    achievement on 97
  of
    conscious evolution 99
    higher evolution 79
    initiation 99
    def. 98
  obstacles on 79
Paul, the Apostle 172
peace 242
peak experiences 107
people, free, rela. to health 264
perfection
  def. 258
  urge to progress to 241
permanent atoms,
see atoms, permanent
Persia, Jesus in 70

physical body,
see body, physical
picture 210
Pilate 152
P(p)lan, (The) 15, 16, 17, 228
   for this planet 17
   Formation of 15
   of the Hierarchy 149
   purpose rela. to 15
   rela. to Intuitional Plane 148
   symbol of 24
   unfolding 11
   vision and for humanity 198
P(p)lane(s)
   astral, purification of 223
   atomic 145
   etheric
     and Cosmic substance 145
     fourth, webs within 174
     planes between 174
   mental, lower 223
   webs between 174
planet
   creation of 15
   our 26
   Plan for this 17
Planetary Life, webs in the 177
Planetary Logos, Will of our 201
Plato 22
poisonous gases,
see gases, poisonous
polarization 218
politicians
   will be philosophers 225
politics, freedom in 259
pollution 224, 228
posthypnotic suggestion,
see suggestion, posthypnotic
pralaya 73
prayer 231
pregnant woman (women),
see woman (women), pregnant
Presence
   and meditator 240
   The Almighty 12
Priesthood 255

problems 227, 238, 239, 245
   def. 240
   suppression of 239
   with delinquency 60
progress
   of humanity 57
   on the mental plane
     rela. to sublimation 222
   urge to 241
promised land 80
protection 210
   shield of 221
psychiatrists 176
psychic people, def. 241
psychism, lower 223
   a cause of 179
psychologists 176
purification 23, 101, 102, 249
   of the astral plane 223
purity, def. 274
Purpose 15
   divine 232
   and Will 148
   def. 148
   for this solar system 147
   in Shamballa 149
   of the Creator 12
   Registrants of the 148
   rela. to Plan 15
   thinking about 237
pyramid of Egypt 20
Pythagoras
   rela. to Master K.H. 159

Q

quality
   thinking about 229, 231, 237
questions 225, 232, 241

R

radiation, effects of 179
radioactivity 176, 224
Rainbow Bridge 58
R(r)ay(s)
  Cosmic 65, 180
  Second 18
  Sixth 18
Rebirth, Law of,
see Law of Rebirth
Registrants of the Purpose 148
relation(s)
  between matter and spirit 85
  right human 207
R(r)eligion(s) 18
  inspired from same source 87
  New World 212
religious fanatics,
see fanatics, religious
rents
  causes of 176
  in planetary veils 180
  in veils 173
  results of 176
renunciation 105
responsibility, sense of 224
righteousness
  def. 274
  Teacher of 67
Rod of Power 201
Room, The Upper 123
rulers of the world 225

S

sacrament(s) 255
  of Baptism 66
  of Holy Communion 66
Sanat Kumara 12, 16, 84
  and Shamballa 148
  Will of 149
sanity and mental health 221
Satan 79

Saul of Tarsus 172
Saviors 13
S(s)chools 66
  mystery 18, 19
  rela. to change of nation 62
S(s)cience 261
  of becoming Oneself 18
  of Telepathy 233
scientists 25, 224
seed(s)
  in the Chalice 146
  thought 231
Self
  -actualization
    and meditation 237
  transpersonal 217
  true 276
sense, common
  a cause of losing 221
separatism, how to conquer 271
Sermon on the Mount 114
servers 233
S(s)ervice 101, 233, 249
  def. 249, 274
  sacrificial 25
  selfless, sacrificial 249
  when starts 105
sexual energy, see energy, sexual
Shamballa
  Christ as member of 201
  Council in
    Sanat Kumara and 148
  def. 201
  energy of, release of 120
  Purpose in 149
shield of protection 221
sickness(es) 211
  def. 258
simplicity 224
sin 128
sincerity of Jesus 71
situation, economic 101
slavery 67, 238, 258
Solar Angel 79
Solar Logos 15, 147, 148
solar system, see system, solar

solemnity, def. 274
S(s)oul(s) 255
  advanced 31
  communication
    of 240
    with 255
  conscious, becoming 102
  contact 232
  human, goal of 236
  in man is the inner Christ 212
  infusion 240
  of the Universe 85
  possessing his vehicle 56
  sounds on the battlefield 180
Spark(s) 75
  of Will Power 19
speech
  def. 276
  free 276
  seven qualities of 276
sphere, fiery 98
spine, base of, triple fire at 107
spirits 275
Spiritual Triad 20, 232
  def. 106
spiritual man, see man, spiritual
star 50
stone 79
story of thinking 225
striving 233
  def. 20
  sublimation 245
  causing 218
  progress rela. to 222
Succession, Apostolic 255
suggestion, post-hypnotic
  drugs and 239
sun, rising 79
suppression
  of glamors 211
  of problems, result of 239
sword, not peace 23
symbol(s) 19, 49
  never die away 27
  of the Plan 24
  protection of 26

  unfoldment of 26
S(s)ystem(s)
  nervous
    effects of thought on 241
  Solar 18
    divine Purpose for this 147
    making the grade in 73
    pralaya between 73

T

T(t)eacher(s) 30
  among humanity 22
  G(g)reat 244
    message of the 30
    purpose of 23
  of Righteousness 67
Teaching (The)
  crystallization in 30
  effects of in world 113
  new 30
    enemies to 30
  of Christ 257
  purpose of 118
  of the Hierarchy 32
Telepathy, Science of 233
T(t)emple(s) 22
  Inner 80
  veil of the 171
temptations 94
Teraphim 52
"The Sons of Men are One" 126
thinker(s) 219, 225
  deeper 224
  interest of 224
thinking, 225, 227
  about cause 236
  about form 237
  creative, 226, 228
  def. 220, 226
  on low levels 222
  rela. to meditation 231
  rela. to mental levels 234
  result of 225

right, effects of 231
three principal ways of 223
thought
  cause of 62
  effects of 241
  energy and centers 244
Tibet 69
Torch of the Ages 11
T(t)ransfiguration 220
  Initiation, def. 102
  transformation 218, 220, 221
  and meditation 218
  of human being
    rela. to meditation 218
  of nature of man 18
  process 177
transmutation 219
  agents of 25
  of nature of man 18
tree, Christ as 49
triangles 179
tuning fork 221

U

unity 175
Universe 75
  mystery behind 18
  Soul of the 85
Upper Room 123, 126
upset 246
urge
  hypnotic 221
  to progress to perfection 241

V

values 212
vehicles
  lower, conquest of our 237
  preparation of 55

subtle
  forces or energies rela. to 61
veil(s) 175, 212
  and webs, rela. between 177
  between planes 180
  ethers rela. to 177
  of
    aspiration 172
    distortion 171
    impulsion 170
    the temple 171
  planetary 173
    rents in 180
  protectiveness of 173
  Rending the 169
  rents in the 173
  separating Halls 169
victory 80
viewpoints
  four 230, 234, 236, 242
Virgo 49
virtues, and freedom 268
vision(s) 15
  and plan for humanity 198
  cause of 62
  for humanity 198
  mysteries rela. to 18
  of the New Age 126
Vyasa 22

W

war 67, 178, 190
washing of the feet 129
water, symbol of 101, 125
way to Christ 217
web(s) 175
  between planes 174
  etheric 175
  of the planet 178
  in the planetary Life 177
  rela. to consciousness
    175, 176

rending
  Christ and Buddha and 180
Wesak Full Moon of 1975 120
Wilderness, In The 89
Will, (the)
  Custodians of 148
  Divine Purpose and 148
  divine 40, 127, 248
    origin of 148
  fire of 20
  of
    God 248
    our Planetary Logos 201
    Sanat Kumara 149
    the Almighty One 17
  Power, Spark of 19
"Wine" of the Spiritual Will 129
Wisdom of Ages, classes in 107
withdrawal from bodies 247
woman, pregnant 56, 58, 59, 60
Word(s)
  Lost, def. 74
  of Power 95
work, our individual 86
worries 267
worship, centers of 18

Y

yoga, hatha 176

Z

Zechariah 79
Zoroaster 22

ABOUT THE AUTHOR

Torkom Saraydarian was born in Asia Minor. Since his childhood he tried to understand the mystery called man.

He visited monasteries, ancient temples, and mystery schools in order to find the answers to his burning questions.

He lived with sufis, dervishes, Christian mystics, and with teachers of occult lore. It took long years of discipline and sacrifice to absorb the Ageless Wisdom from its true sources. Meditation became a part of his daily life and service a natural expression of his soul.

He has lectured in many cities; he has forty-four published books and many articles in occult, philosophical, and religious publications.

He is a violinist, a teacher, a lecturer, a mechanical engineer, meteorologist, writer, and philosopher.

Christ, The Avatar of Sacrificial Love is written to show the uniqueness of Christ, as the World Teacher, as the Path leading to the brotherhood of men, and to the innermost Reality within man and the Universe.

Other Books by Torkom Saraydarian

The Ageless Wisdom
The Bhagavad Gita
Breakthrough to Higher Psychism
Challenge For Discipleship
Christ The Avatar of Sacrificial Love
A Commentary on Psychic Energy
Cosmic Shocks
Cosmos in Man
Dialogue With Christ
Dynamics of Success
Earthquakes and Disasters
Flame of Beauty, Culture, Love, Joy
The Flame of the Heart
Hiawatha and the Great Peace
The Hidden Glory of the Inner Man
Hierarchy and The Plan
I Was
Irritation, the Destructive Fire
Joy and Healing
Legend of Shamballa
New Dimensions in Healing
Olympus, World Report — The Year 3000
Other Worlds
The Psyche and Psychism
The Psychology of Cooperation and Group
    Consciousness
The Purpose of Life
The Science of Becoming Oneself
The Science of Meditation
The Sense of Responsibility in Society
Sex, Family, and the Woman in Society

The Solar Angel
Spiritual Regeneration
Spring of Prosperity
The Subconscious Mind and The Chalice
Symphony of the Zodiac
Talks on Agni
Triangles of Fire
The Unusual Court
Woman, Torch of the Future
The Year 2000 & After

Booklets

A Daily Discipline of Worship
Building Family Unity
Fiery Carriage and Drugs
Five Great Mantrams of the New Age
The Psychology of Cooperation
Questioning Traveler and Karma
Responsibility
The Responsibility of Fathers
The Responsibility of Mothers
Synthesis
Torchbearers
What to Look for in the Heart of Your Partner

Video

The Seven Rays Interpreted

Music Cassette Tapes

Dance of The Zodiac
Far Horizons
Fire Blossom
Infinity
Lao Tse
Light Years Ahead
Lily in Tibet
Misty Mountains
Rainbow
Spirit of My Heart
Sun Rhythms
Tears of My Joy
Torkom Saraydarian Piano Compositions
Toward Freedom

Correspondence Courses

Under the supervision of Torkom Saraydarian, the Aquarian Educational Group offers meditation correspondence courses that are based on the science of meditation, leading the student step-by-step into the practical application of meditation.

The courses we offer are:

a) Reflective Reading courses
b) The Woman Course
c) Meditation, the Creative Process Course
d) *The Bhagavad Gita* Course
e) Discipleship Course
f) *Secret Doctrine* Course
g) Advanced Course

All these courses may be available to the student with the needed qualifications.

We believe that every individual can unfold and release his or her inner potentials by striving toward perfection through meditation, study, and service.

▲

Ordering Information

Write to the Aquarian Educational Group, P.O. Box 267, Sedona, AZ 86339 for additional information regarding:

- ▲ Catalog of author's books and music tapes
- ▲ Public lecture series by Torkom Saraydarian on video and audio cassette tapes
- ▲ Correspondence Courses
- ▲ Seminars

▲

The Aquarian Educational Group

is an educational and religious tax-exempt organization dedicated to right human relations, goodwill, the enlightenment of the mind, and the development of the heart through education, the arts, and the study of world scriptures.

Classes are held at our Centers in Sedona, Arizona, and in Agoura, California. We also hold monthly seminars and Sun-sign festivals at both Centers. Our lectures, seminars, and festivals are dedicated to philosophy, psychology, science, religion, and culture.

We offer home study courses on scientific meditation and world scriptures; we publish many educational and religious books and pamphlets. We also offer baptisms, weddings, Last Rites, and Holy Communion.

Special counselling and lectures are provided for those who need help in overcoming their habits of using marijuana, drugs, or those who need family counselling. Please contact us if we can be of service to you.

All our services are provided through contributions.

Please send your correspondence and contributions to:

Aquarian Educational Group
P.O. Box 267
Sedona, AZ 86339
United States of America

TEL: (602) 282-2655
FAX: (602) 282-0514

▲

The Great Invocation

From the point of Light within the Mind of God
Let light stream forth into the minds of men
Let Light descend on Earth.

From the point of Love within the Heart of God
Let love stream forth into the hearts of men
May Christ return to Earth.

From the center where the Will of God is known
Let purpose guide the little wills of men —
the Purpose which the Masters know and serve.

From the center which we call the race of men
Let the Plan of Love and Light work out
and may it seal the door where evil dwells.

Let Light and Love and Power
restore the Plan on Earth.

▲